Residential child care in practice

Making a difference

Mark Smith, Leon Fulcher and Peter Doran

First published in Great Britain in 2013 by

The Policy Press
University of Bristol
Fourth Floor
Beacon House
Queen's Road
Bristol BS8 1QU
UK
t: +44 (0)117 331 4054
f: +44 (0)117 331 4093
tpp-info@bristol.ac.uk
www.policypress.co.uk

North American office:
The Policy Press
c/o The University of Chicago Press
1427 East 60th Street
Chicago, IL 60637, USA
t: +1 773 702 7700
f: +1 773 702 9756
sales@press.uchicago.edu
www.press.uchicago.edu

British Library Cataloguing in Publication Data
A catalogue record for this book is available from the British Library.

Library of Congress Cataloging-in-Publication Data
A catalog record for this book has been requested.

ISBN 978 1 84742 310 8 paperback
ISBN 978 1 84742 311 5 hardcover

Cover design by The Policy Press.
Front cover: image kindly supplied by www.istock.com
Printed and bound in Great Britain by Hobbs, Southampton.
The Policy Press uses environmentally responsible print partners.

FSC
www.fsc.org
MIX
Paper from
responsible sources
FSC® C020438

Contents

About the authors

Mark Smith is senior lecturer in social work at the University of Edinburgh. Prior to that he lectured in social work at the University of Strathclyde, where he established the MSc in advanced residential child care. Before moving to academia he was a practitioner and manager in residential care settings over a period of 20 years. He has written extensively on residential child care and is particularly interested in the nature of care and in ideas of upbringing.

Leon Fulcher has worked for more than 40 years as a social worker in residential child and youth care work and foster care and as a university teacher across several parts of the world. Leon has specialised in working across cultures and geographies, team working and caring for caregivers, as well as supervision and promoting learning with adult carers.

Peter Doran has worked in and managed residential care and education services throughout his 34-year career in social work. Now semi-retired, he has undertaken work on fostering and permanence for a local authority and chaired a national review of services for children and young people with complex additional support needs for the Scottish government.

Acknowledgements

We would like to record our thanks to Dave Crimmens who offered comments on earlier drafts of the book and to the series editors for their sustained support.

Foreword

These days it requires considerable courage to write a book about residential group care. And it requires a sort of 'realist idealism' to write one that doesn't demand that residential programmes produce measurable outcomes and clinical transformations in response to the latest evidence base. The very idea of residential group care is under attack in almost every OECD jurisdiction. This kind of care for our most vulnerable children and young people is said to be expensive, ineffective and in violation of what is recognised nearly universally as the good family values. In and of itself, the critique levelled against residential group care is not entirely unreasonable: it is true that there are many residential programmes that seem profoundly unhelpful to young people and their families, and that in some cases even seem to make things considerably worse. And it is certainly true that in many residential programmes the core concepts of family values are nowhere to be found. Far too many young people are growing up in institutional settings, under the oppressive weight of institutional rules and within the overwhelmingly rejecting discourses of conformity, compliance and control. But this is only one part of the story about residential group care; the more interesting parts, and the more hopeful parts, are rarely told.

There are at least two deeply embedded traditions in residential group care that make it difficult to ensure the wellbeing and developmental growth of young people. The first is that we have come to believe that residential care is to be used as a last resort only. Here the logic is that given the disadvantages of residential group care relative to what can be offered to young people in a family context (attachment issues, challenges associated with group living, institutional cultures), and furthermore given the unconvincing outcome data of residential group care, young people who cannot grow up at home should be given every opportunity to find success in 'family-like settings'. This has traditionally meant foster care, but now also includes the increasing focus on kinship care in most jurisdictions. There is, of course, great value in these kinds of generalised principles, and indeed many young people have benefitted immeasurably from their placements in family-like settings. As is always the case, however, generalised principles with assumed universal applicability produce as many challenges as they resolve. The implementation of such principles, guided by tight policy environments that seek to balance the quality of care with economic considerations, has been at best mediocre and sometimes tragically comic. What else can one conclude about common practices of placement shuffles, by the end of which some young people will have experienced ten, fifteen and sometimes more 'family-like' environments, in addition to countless school moves, peer group replacements, and 'evidence-based psychotherapeutic services'?

The net impact of the residential group care avoidance strategy currently in vogue is twofold. On the one hand, young people finally admitted to residential group care have already experienced multiple losses, failures and abandonments on top of the original issues they may have encountered within their birth families. As a result, their cynicism, scepticism and ultimately their resistance to whatever is offered in residential group care are quite reasonably at very high levels. On the other hand, if there is one thing we know for certain in relation to residential group care, it is that this is not an easy place for young people to live, to grow up and to form their identities. At a time of great instability in their lives, young people are asked to accept living with six or more strangers of similar age who themselves have encountered multiple challenges in their lives, and they are to be cared for by multiple caregivers – often as many as fifteen different individuals per week. They are to find comfort in what far too often are unsuitable physical environments, among neighbours who reject their presence, and with expectations of performance that typically far exceed those placed on young people living relatively normal, family-based lives. Young people placed in residential group care are to do all of this while coming to terms with any number of mental health challenges, learning disabilities and attachment deficits.

One might think, quite reasonably, that doing all of this requires excellent social skills, high self-esteem, advanced self-management, and a proven track record of high performance in school, with respect to behaviour and particularly in the context of relationship formation and attachment capacity. Yet, when we examine who is placed in residential group care, we find very quickly that it is precisely those young people who lack in all of these areas. These young people carry with them extensive track records of failed relationships, unfulfilled attachments, serious deficits in social skills, low self-esteem, multiple school failures and a limited ability to deal with challenges to their rights, their value as human beings and their integration in mainstream social relations. In short, placement in residential group care becomes most likely at a time when a young person is least ready for it. If anything, the increasingly universal view of residential group care as placement of last resort has rendered this dynamic more pronounced, more acute and more relevant.

Having spent more than two decades immersed in residential care and treatment, as youth worker, as manager and director, and also as researcher, I have come to the conclusion that the ever-deepening rejection of this form of care giving is a self-fulfilling prophecy. The more we seek to construct residential group care as the problem, the more we intensify its challenges. Several patterns within the broad context of residential group care across many different jurisdictions confirm this point. These include the complacency toward human resource development, the reliance on treatment models and the nearly absolute exclusion of expertise that reflects the knowledge and wisdom of young people and their families in the process of understanding both the challenges faced by young people and the possible paths toward growth and resilience.

The first of these patterns concerns the staffing of residential care facilities.

In many jurisdictions around the world, human resources associated with residential group care are characterised by one massive and utterly scandalous feature: anyone, and I really mean absolutely anyone, can legally work in a group care facility. In Canada, the United States and Australia, for example, there are no legislated or even regulated requirements for pre-service qualifications of residential workers. A person with a pulse (although technically even this is not required) is deemed adequately qualified under current legislative and regulatory regimes to work every day with young people facing histories of severe trauma, a complex web of mental health and personal challenges, and uncertainty about their developmental and social trajectory. This simple fact creates circumstances that are similar to allowing heart surgery to be performed by hobby surgeons, or by people who identify as having a long-standing interest in hearts. It is the equivalent of relying on accountants who showed promise in elementary school arithmetic, or police officers who look good in uniform.

This lack of attention to who really is qualified to work with young people in the extraordinarily complex context of residential group care results in two equally problematic dynamics. First, and perhaps most obviously, it means that there is an inherent mismatch between the needs of young people and the capacity of caregivers to meet those needs; second, and perhaps of greater long-term consequence, service providers are given carte blanche to invent programmes and services and impose the implementation of these on front line workers who are ill equipped to question their merit, and whose primary concern may well be to conform and comply in order to safeguard their employment, for which they know well they aren't really qualified.[1] It comes as no surprise, therefore, that while there has been much talk and rhetoric about the quality of care delivered through residential programmes, the rhetoric is far ahead of the practice in most settings.

This brings us to the second pattern, deeply embedded and ever accelerating in residential group care. This is the pre-eminence of 'treatment' language and approaches that define what actually happens day

---

[1] I should point out that many residential care facilities do require appropriate pre-service qualifications, even if this is not a legislated or regulatory requirement. Not surprisingly, some of the dynamics elaborated here are mitigated in settings where appropriately qualified front line staff are employed most of the time.

to day in these programmes. Under the guise of 'behaviour modification', 'corrective experiences' and 'personal accountability', residential programmes everywhere are imposing deficit-based interventions on vulnerable young people, who are to internalise such externally imposed 'corrections' to their identities and activities. Historically, such interventions were often quite randomly generated, based on the intuitive knowledge of managers and directors, their own value systems of how young people ought to be, or socially mandated strong arm approaches to fixing what were often seen as delinquent youths. To be fair, the motive for 'treatment' has changed over the years, and today we find the imposition of treatment interventions to be not so much random as randomly derived from the evidence for what works. The move to embrace evidence-based practices has both positive and negative features. On the positive side, accountability for doing work that features high fidelity with research studies and methodically articulated intervention approaches has increased significantly, taking out some of the random impositions of power and control in many settings. On the negative side, the humanity of young people, their uniqueness, their differences and their multiple identities have also largely been eliminated. Instead of a concern for young people's experiences every day, residential group care is focused on young people's compliance with how they ought to be and their correspondence with the commands of Plans of Care, performance expectations and 'getting better'. Indeed, whether or not young people themselves experience positive growth and development is largely irrelevant; what does matter is that the assessment tools closely aligned to the interventions show positive results.

The focus on evidence-based practices and the corresponding assessment tools has had two major consequences. First, it has further marginalised front line youth workers inasmuch as their experiences in being with young people produce no recordable data; we don't measure the quality of relationships, the often nuanced changes in the experience of sharing space and experiences, or the enhanced capacities of young people to resist, to rebel and to be reflectively non-compliant. Quite to the contrary, within the evidence-based framework for treatment, these aspects of change are deemed either undesirable or meaningless. What we do measure are the responses young people give on assessment tools, and the degree to which these reflect what the intervention sought to achieve in the first place. The role of front line workers is thus reduced to reporting on and documenting only those developments that are measured on the requisite forms. The whole of being together is fragmented into selective parts, some of which are discarded as irrelevant while others are meticulously recorded as the core factors of treatment success.

The second consequence of evidence-based approaches to treatment is their impact on how these construct everyday life experiences as undifferentiated data informing points of measuring change at regular intervals. Measurement tools necessarily require the categorisation of experiences into manageable categories that can be measured, and that pre-select what the outcome of change should look like. It is notable that there are no evidence-based approaches that seek to generate young people who are rebellious (critical), non-compliant (assertive), non-conforming (socially progressive), and eccentric (unique). One thing I have learned over the years is that especially among young people living in residential group care, we find that many have untapped strengths that simply cannot be rendered congruent with the conservative, conformist and value-laden agendas of treatment based on evidence.

Finally, we arrive at the third embedded pattern in residential group care: the exclusion of young people's voices, the marginalisation of their families and communities, and the discrediting of expertise that is not derived from the quasi-scientific commands of empirical research. Here we also find some of the exquisite ironies associated with residential group care. Much of the evidence, after all, clearly confirms that the outcomes of residential group care are significantly more sustainable if families are directly involved in the everyday care and treatment of young people. Indeed, successful outcomes of residential group care depend substantially on the active involvement of young people themselves in their care plans, as well as the engagement of their families and where possible their communities. Yet it is readily apparent that many residential group care settings are at best hesitant, and more likely resistant, to involving young people and their families in any substantive manner. Instead, the expertise of the evidence-based intervention strategy is thought to override any contributions the consumer of services could possibly make. Their expertise is seen as peripheral, insignificant and likely the reason for the need of service in the first place. Young people and their families are to integrate themselves into and conform to the requirements of the expert-driven intervention. All of this results in the alienation of young people and their families from the services offered by their residential care providers, rendering the whole experience of residential care a coercive one, in which young people endure the interventions but look forward to the day of discharge, when they regain some of the agency they seek over their own lives.

I started this Foreword by speaking to the courage it takes to write yet another book about residential group care. This is a sinking ship in many respects, both because of the prevailing preferences virtually anywhere in the OECD jurisdiction for family-based care and also because of the lack of a cohesive framework for residential group care. And then along comes this book by Smith, Fulcher and Doran. I think this is the kind of writing that can reconfigure the kind of story we might tell about residential group care in the future. Here we find an articulation of how to be present with young people as they face their upbringing every day, moment by moment. The emphasis on relationships, on kindness, on love, on nurture and also on guidance, discipline and learning is exactly what is needed in order to ensure that young people placed in residential group care have the kind of experience that is developmentally appropriate but also personally stimulating and satisfying. The authors prioritise the experience of being with young people over the specific nature of the interventions and treatment approaches imposed on young people. They focus on the interfacing of child and youth care practice (largely articulated from the Canadian perspective) and social pedagogy (with very strong elements of the German tradition of pedagogy). This book demonstrates clearly the complexity of doing this work in a residential context, and also the simplicity of human development that we have been so preoccupied with rendering unnecessarily complicated. As such, the book inadvertently makes the case for ensuring the right people are caring for young people every day, with clarity about the enormous challenges young people face as they are being cared for. Before we look to science, to research, to evidence, let us remember who we are serving in the residential group care context. This work is more than anything else about being with young people, in their everyday experiences, in their lifespace, in their here and now.

Kiaras Gharabaghi
11 June 2012

Introduction

'There were people who really cared and that shone through; and there were people who didn't care and that also shone through.' (David, in Cree and Davis, 2007: 87)

This book is about the care of children in residential settings: children's homes, residential schools, some hospital wards, through to secure accommodation where children and young people are held in physically secure conditions. Residential child care is described as 'a physical setting in which children and young people are offered care – physical nurturing, social learning opportunities, the promotion of health and wellbeing and specialized behaviour training' (Fulcher, 2001: 418). Steckley and Smith (2011) argue that moral and relational considerations are also central to how care is offered and experienced; the giving and receiving of care happen at instrumental but also emotional levels, in what is done and in how it is done, as the quote that introduces this chapter might suggest. Children in care know those who they experience as caring for them – and those they don't. We attempt, in this volume, to develop a broad and holistic conception of care: practical, moral and relational.

Care is enacted less in grand policy pronouncements than in what de Certeau (1984) calls the practices of everyday life. The book is about everyday practices of care, illuminated through case scenarios. But everyday practices are located within wider political contexts and are informed by particular professional assumptions and ways of thinking about, for instance, children and childhood and how best to bring children up – what might be thought of as broad moral or philosophical concerns. So the various chapters of the book encourage readers to be aware of and informed by big ideas in order to inform their practice in the local or everyday. But first, this introductory chapter sets a context for such practice by charting changing understandings of care over time and by setting out the theoretical orientations we find helpful in conceptualising and practising residential child care.

A brief history of residential child care

A Dickensian image of the Victorian workhouse casts a long shadow over residential child care, not only in its portrayal of brutish custodians presiding over hapless orphans but also, less obviously perhaps, because it exemplifies the Poor Law doctrine of less eligibility. This was intended to prevent categories of what were perceived to be undeserving poor gaining access to the workhouses. It was thought that to have allowed them to do so would encourage indolence. State care, as a result, was deliberately constructed as austere and unwelcoming, associated with individual failure: a last resort for desperate individuals and families. Residential care has struggled ever since to cast off a residual sense of being considered a last resort, and the stigma that accompanies this.

But residential child care in Victorian times and beyond consisted of far more than workhouses. In response to the social problems caused by industrialisation and urbanisation, philanthropists established children's homes of various shapes and sizes across the length and breadth of Britain. They also turned their attention to questions of juvenile delinquency, establishing industrial and reformatory schools. The motivation behind most such initiatives, certainly from the mid-19th century onwards, was a sense of 'rescuing' children from parents and families that were considered to be contaminating influences. Victorian philanthropy was rarely entirely benign, though, and genuine concern for children was often conflated with fears around social order and concerns for the 'souls' and social standing of individual philanthropists (Butler and Drakeford, 2005).

Throughout the 19th century and for much of the 20th century, state care was focused on the provision of children's basic needs for food, shelter and cleanliness, a position reified in the 1908 Children Act. Care was, essentially, seen as a mothering role; the gendered nature of this assumption reflected in the fact that children's homes were generally run by 'godly women', often spinsters who devoted their lives to this role. There was also an emphasis on building character, to be achieved through austerity, hard work and religious instruction. The goal was to prepare young people for gainful employment, often in military or domestic service, and to prevent them becoming a burden on the state. Children's emotional life was rarely acknowledged in the way we might nowadays seek to understand it. In fact, to pander to it might have been considered detrimental to their moral upbringing (Smith, 2012).

The 1920s saw a growth in psychological ideas, which slowly started to influence ways of thinking about child rearing. These percolated into the child guidance movement, run by psychologists and psychiatric social workers. The child guidance movement, in turn, started to have an impact on child care policy over the course of the 1930s and 1940s. The 1946 Curtis and Clyde Committees, in England and Scotland respectively, criticised large scale institutional care and recommended that children should be looked after in small family-based homes in order that their emotional as well as their physical needs might be addressed. These reports led to the 1948 Children Act, which established Children's Committees in every local authority. While practices were no doubt variable and, by the standards of another day, might be considered questionable, Webb (2010) identifies a sense of purpose and vocation among those who ran children's homes, many of which remained under the management of churches or charities, large and small. A number of therapeutic communities also emerged around this period, offering psychologically informed planned environments designed to address a wide range of children's needs. From the 1940s to the 1980s therapeutic communities provided progressive – often theoretically robust and largely successful – care and education to those children placed there. They fell foul of the general shift away from residential care over the course of the 1980s and, perhaps, a sense that they operated outside the mainstream of provision.

The identification of the family as the model for institutional care in the 1948 Children Act led to the growth from the 1950s of family group homes, in which live-in 'aunties' and 'uncles' brought up groups of children alongside their own families. A similar model emerged in residential schools, where housemasters and housemothers were responsible for and lived attached to cottage units in which the children lived. Reflecting wider societal attitudes at that time, gender roles remained fairly well defined, with the 'auntie' or housemother taking responsibility for domestic and nurturing tasks and the 'uncle' or housemaster expected to take on a disciplinary role.

Residential child care within social work

Legislation in the late 1960s led to the professionalisation of social work. Social work was to be 'generic', bringing together all client groups within unitary social work departments. The Central Council for Education and Training in Social Work declared that residential child care was to be considered part of the new social work profession – a position that did not meet with universal approval, especially from teachers who, until that point, had been the dominant professional group in residential schools.

Social work, as it developed following the seminal legislation of the late 1960s, drew on two dominant strands of thinking. The first of these had a clinical orientation, deriving from the medical roots that formed one thread in the profession's history, focusing on individual and family problems. The second strand was an increasingly structural perspective, drawing on a literature hostile to institutional care. Goffman's (1968) *Asylums* is perhaps the foremost example of this, and it can still be applied uncritically to residential child care settings (for example, Green and Masson, 2002) even although current day homes and schools are far from Goffman's portrayal of the 'total institution'. Both these strands of thinking – the individual clinical and the anti-institutional – highlight some ambivalence and tensions in conceptualising residential child care within social work (Milligan, 1998; Anglin, 1999; Fulcher, 2003).

Ambivalence towards residential child care was reflected in a strong preference for fostering as the placement of choice for children who could not be cared for at home. The *Children who wait* report (Rowe and Lambert, 1973), commissioned by the Association of British Adoption Agencies and influenced by the growing literature around attachment (Bowlby, 1951), claimed that all children need to be brought up in a family environment. It identified thousands of children in residential care settings, many of whom did not need to be there, and an absence of planning for their futures. In that sense, it cast a necessary spotlight on local authorities' child care practices.

Children who wait also came to be used, however, to support a more ideological case that residential child care could not provide sufficiently strong attachment opportunities or the experience of permanence for children (Milligan, 1998). The assumption that alternative family care was the preferred choice for children became deeply embedded in social work thinking. *Changing lives*, the report of the 21st Century Social Work Review in Scotland (Scottish Executive, 2006), reflects a wider social work orthodoxy when it notes, without further explanation or evidence, that 'While residential child care remains the option of choice for a few children, many more are accommodated in residential provision due to a shortage of foster placements' (2006: 23). Foster care was also considered to be a cheaper option.

Despite such strong professional preference for foster care, there is growing evidence that, as it has been used within local authority social work as a short-term measure, it does not provide stability for many of the children placed there. Indeed, in many cases it can build instability, as children are moved serially between foster placements. Frampton (2004) makes a strong case, built upon his experience of having been brought up a 'Dr Barnardo's boy', for the merits of residential care over foster care.

The professionalisation of social work and the inclusion of residential child care within it meant that the nature of care changed from what had been a largely domestic task to become a more ostensibly professional one. Professionalisation saw a shift away from the live-in staff who had been at the heart of previous models of care to what Douglas and Payne (1981) call an 'industrial model', in which the personal and professional selves of carers became separated. This was brought about, on the one hand, by structural changes such as the introduction of shift systems, but also by ideas that made particular assumptions of what it was to be 'professional'. Specifically, the notion of 'care' became downplayed in a profession that set out its stall around encouraging qualities of independence and empowerment. Social work, in the view of some commentators, considered itself 'so tainted by its associations with care that the word should be expunged from its lexicon and its rationale' (Meagher and Parton, 2004: 4).

Although residential child care was asserted to be part of social work, relationships remained ambivalent. A status and qualifications gap opened up, or at least continued, between what was considered the primarily 'blue collar' task of direct care and the increasingly 'white collar' task of field social work. This was and continues to be reflected in poorer levels of education and pay among residential workers compared to other welfare professionals. The status differential is also reflected in the management systems that have grown up around residential care, where workers are not considered to be educated as autonomous professionals and therefore require close supervision within hierarchical external management structures.

In the UK, the 1989 Children Act and the 1995 Children (Scotland) Act reinforced shifting conceptions of care. These pieces of legislation reflected a move towards more legalistic and contractual approaches to service provision. They replaced the term 'in care' with that of 'looked after' to describe children and young people in the care of the state. Children and young people in residential care are described as being 'looked after and accommodated', suggesting an instrumental and short-term conception of care – a hotelling function – rather than the open-ended, if arguably unfocused, commitment that had gone before.

At a wider level social work was also changing, away from what had been, primarily, a family welfare service, to one increasingly concerned with child protection where the aim was to target 'problem' or 'dangerous' families for intervention (Parton, 1985). This shift in orientation facilitated what Holman calls 'a different kind of social work which (is) at once both mechanical and inspectorial – some would say macho. Social workers found themselves having to follow procedures contained in rule books which were almost the size of novels' (1998: 124).

This trend towards increasingly procedural practice was a feature of the political and economic doctrines of managerialism (Clarke and Newman, 1997). Managerial regimes were based around notions of economy, efficiency and effectiveness, and a belief that these aims could be achieved by more and better management (Pollitt, 1993). Managerialism's imprint on practice became apparent in ideas that care could be broken down into clean-cut notions of assessment and programmed interventions that would lead to measurable and improved outcomes. Rose identifies the experience of care for 'looked after' children within a contemporary social work paradigm, noting that:

> Short-term outcomes are the order of the day, with a requirement
> for focused pieces of work that can be added to the list of 'jobs

done' and performance measures achieved. The rationale for much of this is shrouded in the perceived importance of evidence-based approaches and a reliance on quasi-scientific methodologies to justify short-term interventions that also, conveniently, meet the need for being cost effective. (2010: 1–2)

A consequence of this push for measurable outcomes from care has, according to Halvorsen been that 'one is in danger of giving a child's fundamental need for care a lower priority' (2009: 79).

A combination of ideology and cost contributed substantially to the decline in the usage of residential child care from a high point in the mid-1970s (Bebbington and Miles, 1989). In England, for instance, 'placements in community homes fell from over 25,000 to less than 2,000 between 1981 and 2000' (Kendrick, 2012: 288), with similar falls evident across the different countries of the UK and also in different sectors such as residential schools. The age profiles of children in residential care show how younger children are less frequently placed there, with the result that what is offered is, predominantly, a service for adolescents. Any service catering for groups of adolescents might be thought to pose a challenge to carers. Courtney and Iwaniec (2009) identify how it is often only the most troubled, challenging and hard to place children and young people who are placed in residential care; it has, in many respects, become a residual service. This has inevitable implications for group dynamics. There are fewer 'culture carriers' who might, previously, have been relied upon to set a reasonably settled tone within a group, thus highlighting issues of behaviour management.

The recent history of residential child care

The history of residential child care since the 1980s has been a chequered one, characterised by continuing ideological aversion to its use, perceptions of poor outcomes and a series of child abuse scandals, which first came to light over the course of the 1990s (Smith, 2009). All of these reinforce a particularly negative perception of the sector.

Evidence to support such negative views is, however, rarely clear cut. Debate about the seemingly poor outcomes of residential child care needs to be conducted against the backdrop of the changing population, whereby only the most difficult to place young people end up there, rendering comparison with the wider population of children problematic. And, while residential child care may not be as good as it might be, evidence of poor outcomes is, in fact, far less clear than can be suggested. Forrester (2008) and Forrester et al (2009) show that being admitted into care (both foster and residential) almost always leads to some improvement in children's personal and social situations. Focusing on views of care being bad for children results in a tendency to further restrict its use, and thus deny the most vulnerable group of children in our society the advantages that care provision can bring (Forrester et al, 2009).

The abuse scandals that have engulfed residential child care over the past 20 years are discussed in a series of inquiry reports (see Corby et al, 2001; Sen et al, 2008). The biggest of all the inquiries, the Waterhouse (2000) report into abuse in children's homes and residential schools in North Wales, had a major impact on policy and practice in relation to residential child care as care providers were faced with implementing its wide range of recommendations. Yet, despite the emotion and publicity that questions around abuse in care generate, questions can also be asked of its assumed extent. Webster (2005), for instance, offers a compelling deconstruction of the Waterhouse report, upon which many of the assumptions of widespread abuse are based, while Gallagher (2000) raises questions as to whether abuse was more common in residential child care than in any other setting – such as teaching, youth work or foster care – where adults have contact with children. Smith (2010a) and Smith et al (2012) question the epistemological basis upon which understandings of abuse are constructed. This is undoubtedly a complicated and emotive issue that merits ongoing academic debate. Its primary relevance for this volume stems from the fundamental impact that assumptions of abuse and the measures taken to address it have had on everyday care in respect of risk-averse practices. Some of this impact is addressed at points within the book.

The regulatory reform of social care

The New Labour Government elected in the UK in 1997 adopted what it called a 'Third Way' to policy formulation. This was claimed to be an ostensibly modern and efficient approach to government, in which 'what mattered was what worked'. Third Way politics placed great faith in regulation. Specifically, it saw the introduction of legislation to regulate care introduced across all parts of the UK in 2001. This set standards against which care homes might be inspected and also introduced regulation of the workforce. The purpose of this legislation was said to be the improvement of services and safeguarding of the public. McLaughlin (2010) argues that there is little evidence that it has done either. What these developments and the way they have been interpreted and enacted have done is to create an 'enormous proliferation of legislation, regulation and guidance ... as if by classifying, codifying, monitoring, incentivising and target setting in almost every conceivable sphere of social interaction, government could achieve the complete set of beneficial and positive outcomes' (Jordan,

2010: 3). Regulation, thus, has not been an unequivocal force for good in residential child care. It is seen as a burden by many staff and has contributed, fundamentally, to a profusion of paperwork and reporting, often at the expense of direct care practice.

Conceptual problems also arise in respect of the regulatory apparatus as it has developed. While legislation specifies who is to provide care, where, and the penalties for failing to do so, it neglects to say what care might be. Care is conceptualised primarily as a technical and legal endeavour to be evidenced through rafts of procedure and paperwork. But, as the sociologist Bauman observes, when we obscure the essential human and moral aspects of care behind ever more rules and regulations, we make 'the daily practice of social work ever more distant from its original ethical impulse' (2000: 9). By this reckoning, the plethora of rules and regulations that increasingly surround practice are not just minor but necessary irritants, but might be argued to dull the moral impulse to care (Smith, 2011b).

The various policy and professional trends that have been brought to bear on residential child care have contributed to a situation whereby:

> the concept of care within public care for children has been rarely seen as visible ... a narrowing of what we mean by care, a lowering of expectations of what the state can offer in terms of care. Of particular note is the marked contrast between the potential for care within families as centring on control and love, and the optimum expected from state care which is around safekeeping. Care as used in legislation seems to have been emptied of its potential, a dried up expression for how to manage an underclass of disadvantage. (Cameron, 2003: 91–2)

Changing policy directions

There appears to be growing realisation that the regulatory and procedurally driven child protection foci applied to work with children and families are not working. There are signs at the level of both policy and ideas that suggest this needs to change; exemplified, perhaps, in the recent *Munro review of child protection* (Munro, 2011), which calls for a realignment of social work practice away from the predominantly procedural towards more relationally based ways of working. We argue in this book that there is a need for different ways of thinking about how we provide state care for children and offer some ideas as to what a different way might involve. Recent policy directions would seem to support such change.

The Every Child Matters policy agenda in England (2003) and the Getting it Right for Every Child policy agenda in Scotland (GIRFEC, 2005) shifted the focus of planning for children's services away from targeting children and families with particular problems towards providing better support for all families and carers, acknowledging that some children and families require additional support at different points along the way. In many respects, the aim of these policy initiatives has been to promote an idea of parenting, whether familial or corporate. The idea of corporate parenting has become a central one in respect of children in state care. Corporate parenting is considered to operate at different levels, including:

- a statutory duty on all parts of a local authority to cooperate in promoting the welfare of children and young people who are looked after by them, and a duty on other agencies to cooperate with councils in fulfilling that duty;
- coordinating the activities of the many different professionals and carers involved in a child or young person's life, and taking a strategic, child-centred approach to integrated service delivery. (www.celcis.org/ looked_after_children/corporate_parenting/)

The idea of the corporate parent, however, extends beyond a duty placed upon local authorities, to move beyond 'corporate' to 'parenting' identified by Jackson et al (2006) as those actions necessary to promote and support children's development over their journey towards adulthood. Local authorities delegate this function to those providing day-to-day care for the child or young person (Scottish Government, 2008: 9).

In this respect, residential child care workers are charged with operationalising the corporate parenting agenda. They are well positioned to do so, being among the most influential of helpers and enablers in a child's life. The location of the corporate parenting agenda with those undertaking children's daily care is reinforced in policy documents emanating from what was previously the Department of Children, Schools and Families in England. This identifies the importance for children in care to have 'stable, reliable, nurturing relationships with those who care for them and manage their care' (DCSF, 2009: para 27) and the failure of the care system to replicate the kind of relationships that children have with their parents, seeking to support the development of such 'parenting' type relationships for children in care. We hope that the ideas presented in this book might inform carers as they undertake their responsibilities as corporate parents and assist them to do so in a way that foregrounds the development of good personal and nurturing relationships.

A different kind of care

Care does not follow simple formulaic patterns of cause and effect that managerial ways of thinking might like to assume. Successful outcomes are achieved in the messy and non-linear processes in which relationship building and purposeful activity come together to give children and young people optimism about their future life chances. This requires a shift beyond an instrumental focus to consider what are essentially moral questions. Moss and Petrie (2002) suggest three such questions: who are children, what is a good childhood and what kind of relationships do we want to have with children? The idea of a good childhood might find resonances with the ancient Greek philosopher Aristotle's concern for what constitutes a good life, which he associates with a sense of human flourishing or happiness. We propose here that residential child care ought to strive towards a broad idea of children's flourishing and happiness, not merely their safety or their examination results. This demands that care ought to be informed by a sense of moral purpose and direction; it can feel that this has been lost in much policy and practice in recent decades. We now turn to the theoretical orientations that we consider might be useful in working towards such a purpose.

Practice orientations informing the book

Our method in writing this book draws on two main approaches or traditions of practice, which share common features. These are child and youth care and social pedagogy. Our thinking is also informed by ethical perspectives and particularly by the growing interest in care ethics or feminist ethics, ideas from which will be introduced and developed at different points in the book. We believe that, together, such theoretical orientations are consistent with and can help to inform what we identify above as the changing policy agenda.

A child and youth care approach

Child and youth care is the term applied to direct work with children and families across Canada, much of the US and South Africa. While for social workers the 'client' (and his or her 'problems') has become the primary locus of intervention, in child and youth care the focus is on developmental care of children and young people (Anglin, 1999). The early literature on a child and youth care approach has been developed significantly over the past 40 years or so to the point that Garfat and Fulcher (2011) identify 25 characteristics of a child and youth care approach to practice. One key text that informs our writing of this volume is Henry Maier's 'The core of care: essential ingredients for the development of children at home and away from home' (1979), which we refer to at various points.

One of the defining ideas within a child and youth care approach is that of life space or 'lifespace', first identified in the literature by Lewin (1951). Lifespace is the total physical and emotional arena in which workers and young people interact. The main factor distinguishing residential child care from any other kind of work with children is that 'practitioners take as the theatre for their work the actual living situations as shared with and experienced by the child' (Ainsworth, 1981: 234). A classic text setting out a lifespace approach to child and youth care is *The other 23 hours* (Trieschman et al, 1969). The title of this book conveys the relative importance of the hours of the day when children are not involved in formal treatment but which, nevertheless, are replete with opportunities for growth.

Working in the lifespace involves 'entering into, and the caring use of daily life events as they are occurring, for the therapeutic benefit of a child, youth or family' (Garfat, 2002), or 'therapy on the hoof', as Redl (1966) describes it. Garfat (1999) captures the nature of child and youth care in his catchy identification of a key component of the task as being about hanging out and hanging in – hanging out or just being with children and young people as they go about their daily lives and hanging in with them when the going gets tough.

The immediacy of lifespace interventions also creates 'in-the-moment learning opportunities' for a child or young person as he or she is living his or her life. This is not a specialised form of psychotherapeutic helping and healing based on reflective conversations in isolated offices, even though it is important that such conversations might take place. A carer intervenes through purposeful contacts that occur in shared living and learning environments. Residential child or youth care workers are potentially the most influential of helpers. They engage in daily living activities with children or young people, spending more accumulated time – hours and days – with them than all other professionals combined. This provides carers with opportunities to intervene proactively, responsively and relationally in daily living moments to help young people discover and learn new ways of being in the world. Ward (2006) calls this 'opportunity-led work'.

One of the problems with care planning as it has emerged within social work is that it places a disproportionate and unmerited faith in instrumental interventions, often farmed out to external 'experts', rarely appreciating the importance of everyday care. Residential workers often buy into this way of working. Thus, a child might be sent to a youth justice worker for their offending behaviour, a counsellor for work on family relationships and a drugs worker. A child and youth care approach by contrast, focuses on enactment, in the moment that it occurs, providing opportunities for a young person to learn, and to practise new thoughts, feelings and actions in their daily lives. Imagine, for example, a young woman who has difficulty engaging in respectful communication, and for whom the staff team has decided that respectful communication will be a part of her care plan. She might, in some models of intervention, take classes in communication, or visit a therapist to understand why she is acting in such a manner. Residential care workers, however, have opportunities in 'real time' to:

- identify immediately when undesirable communication is occurring, in the moment it is occurring, so that both the young person and the carer know exactly what they are discussing;
- process the feelings, thoughts and memories that are occurring as the young person is in the middle of the communication;
- help the young person learn and practise new ways of communicating under particular circumstances – at meals, bedtime, playing and recreation, or doing chores – 'in the daily life space in which it is lived' (Garfat, in Fulcher and Garfat, 2008: 4).

The words 'everyday events' suggest the routine, the non-technical and the unimportant tasks. Yet it was here, in everyday events, that the child's development and function became impaired and problematic, and it is here that a worker's skill lies in getting the youngster's days to start going right again. One of the hopes of this book is that it encourages workers to focus more directly on daily lifespace practices and relational tasks of caring for children and young people. It is within these daily lifespace encounters that carers nurture developmental living and learning opportunities through the planned uses of daily life events. The more carers focus on learning in the moment, the more powerful their interventions are likely to be.

A social pedagogy approach

In recent years, and in many respects acknowledging the poor state of residential child care in the UK, there has been growing interest in social pedagogy, some variant of which is the model of direct care practice across most of Europe. Much work on introducing and developing social pedagogical ideas for an English-speaking audience has been undertaken by academics at the Thomas Coram Research Unit at the University of London (see Petrie et al, 2006; Cameron and Moss, 2011). Social pedagogy is concerned with bringing up children through broadly social educational means; education being considered in its widest sense. The adoption of a broadly educational, or pedagogic, way of thinking has the attraction of shifting the focus away from a child's psychological deficits towards an emphasis on their growth and development or, more generally, on what is needed to promote their upbringing.

The idea of upbringing is a central one in social pedagogic thinking. In Germany *erzieher*, the term for one type of pedagogue, translates as 'upbringer'. Another German term, *bildung*, while not readily amenable to direct translation, also casts some light on what education in its widest sense might involve. *Bildung* incorporates, but at the same time transcends, traditional teaching and learning to include a sense of character and the moral formation of children as full members of society. Ideas of upbringing and *bildung* encompass all that is required for children to develop into healthy and competent adults. Locating the care of children in state care within an overall concept of upbringing perhaps encapsulates but also avoids the pitfalls and tensions of aligning the task too closely to parenting. While the task of state care is to perform the roles that a good parent would normally perform, carers cannot and should not take on the blood bond involved in actual parenting.

The principles of social pedagogy might seem to offer a more promising paradigm than social work within which to locate essential features of residential child care (see Petrie et al, 2006). Social pedagogic practice happens in the lifespace and generally involves groups. It involves elements of head, heart and hands – intellectual, practical and emotional activity on the part of the worker. It is fundamentally relational, stressing the importance of close relationships between workers and children. An inevitable and healthy crossover of the professional and the personal 'selfs' of the worker is acknowledged as being central to effective caring. Social pedagogic work is a self in action task; it requires that workers continually reflect on what they are doing and why, taking differing contexts into account. In that respect, it is dissonant with the instrumental, procedure-bound and risk-averse cultures of residential child care in the UK.

The articulation and expression of an ethical stance is foundational within social pedagogical theory and practice. This, rather than recourse to abstract rules and principles, might be thought of as 'first practice' from which all else follows. Knowledge and skills are both informed by and feed into a practitioner's developing ethical stance. This notion is encapsulated in the social pedagogical concept of *haltung*, which broadly translates as ethos, mindset or attitude, and describes the extent to which one's actions are congruent with one's values and fundamental beliefs (Eichsteller and Holthoff, 2010). *Haltung* incorporates a practitioner's orientation to 'the other' and might revolve around fundamental philosophical questions concerning how they think about others, what kind of relationships they want to have with others and what might be considered to be a good life or a life lived well. A pedagogue's *haltung* is intrinsic to their 'self'. It is that 'self' that the pedagogue utilises in working with others and that contributes to the development of suitably close and authentic relationships.

Child and youth care and social pedagogy both stress the importance of the personal/professional relationship in direct helping work. Relationship-based practice was historically at the heart of social work, but has been marginalised within the case management and managerial regimes that have dominated over recent years. It is, however, enjoying something of a revival across different areas of social work (Ruch et al, 2010; Hennessey, 2011). It is fundamental to residential child care.

The importance of caring relationships is something that few in social work would openly disagree with but there is a danger that asserting the importance of relationships becomes a warmly persuasive but largely empty word or phrase. Putting relationships at the heart of practice challenges current ideas about risk and what might be thought to be 'professional', often associated with qualities of objectivity and detachment (Meagher and Parton, 2004). According to Fewster (1991), there is a need to ensure the experience of intimacy and connectedness in caring relationships while maintaining appropriate boundaries. The trouble in current climates is that we confuse boundaries with barriers – boundaries are individual and personal; barriers reactive and impermeable. Fewster concludes that practitioners should reject professional exhortations to put objectivity before experience and come to recognise that what they bring to the caring role as individuals is of more significance than what might be thought of as professional role behaviour.

Distilling the central features of residential child care

Central features distilled from the child and youth care and social pedagogical literature thread throughout this book. These are the importance of the everyday in caring for children and young people and the conscious use of everyday life events to help promote their growth and development; a lifespace approach. We also identify the limitations of overly procedural and regulatory approaches to care. The importance of relationships is reinforced, acknowledging the need to ensure essential intimacy and connection, while maintaining appropriate personal and professional boundaries. Maintaining boundaries appropriate to particular relationships and contexts is likely to be best ensured through the encouragement of reflective practices on the part of workers and the development of healthy practice cultures rather than through procedural injunction.

A few words about the way the book is organised

Like all books in the *Social Work: Making a Difference* series, this volume is structured around a problem–based learning approach. Practice scenarios provide a way in for readers to explore particular chapter themes. The chapter themes are consistent with current policy directions in respect of children, particularly Every Child Matters in England, Getting It Right for Every Child in Scotland and the Agenda for Children's Services in Ireland. Taken together, the chapters develop an approach to corporate parenting or upbringing within the specific context of residential child care.

The scenarios we have chosen draw upon the authors' experiences in the field. They reflect, as far as possible within the limitations of word count and personal experience, the richness and the complexity of residential child care practice and the knowledge, skills and values involved in practising effectively within it. Following the case examples we draw on relevant policy and theory to provide a discussion around the themes that emerge from each chapter, acknowledging that there is inevitable crossover of themes across chapters. We then return to the case scenarios, considering what might be going on within them. Each chapter then offers some thoughts on how ideas introduced might be brought to bear on practice. Finally, some further reading suggestions are identified.

Our goal has been to write a practice volume that is theoretically sound, but still of practical assistance to those who share lifespaces with children and young people in care. The scenarios and the practice tips are intended to spark thinking and discussion rather than to provide a blueprint for some 'best practice' that we are not sure exists. The best practitioners can aspire to, we believe, is reflective and responsive practice whereby they reflect upon what might be going on in a particular situation, what they themselves bring to it and how they might best respond to what is going on for the child or children.

Further reading

Unlike many social work texts, Martin Davies' recent book offers comprehensive coverage of residential child care:

Davies, M. (ed) (2012) *Social work with children and families,* Basingstoke: Palgrave Macmillan.

Our other suggestions for further reading are for websites:

www.cyc-net.org

is an impressive resource on child and youth care related material and has a helpful search facility;

www.childrenwebmag.com focuses more on UK child care and has some excellent historical material;

www.socialpedagogyuk.com

provides a growing repository of material about social pedagogy.

2

Safe and secure: a sense of belonging

Scenario

Michael is a 12-year-old white boy and was placed in a small children's home due to his parents' inability to care for him. Both parents are drug and alcohol dependent and despite support from the social work team and family support workers they have consistently struggled to meet his physical and emotional needs. Michael was frequently left to care for himself and was often seen wandering the streets late in the evening. He looked ragged and neighbours reported he was often hungry and begging for food and money outside local shops. His school attendance was haphazard and other children called him names because of his unkempt appearance and bullied him. Neighbours and school staff describe Michael as isolated and timid. He has rarely been seen to smile and seems very unhappy.

Michael has been in the children's home for three days. His parents have phoned but have not visited. Long-term plans are unclear. Michael presents as quiet and watchful. He does not engage much with the other four children of a similar age and has spent all his time watching television. He is reluctant to engage in conversation with staff. For each of his three nights in the children's home he has found great difficulty settling at bedtime. He likes a bedtime story but as soon as the worker leaves and turns out his light he gets up, switches the light back on and lies on the floor wrapped in his duvet. He goes to sleep lying on the floor. Workers have tried various approaches to get him into his bed and to switch the light off. Each of these attempts has been met with resistance – at times aggression and at other times whining and toddler-like temper tantrums.

The staff group has discussed strategies to manage the bedtime issues. The senior residential worker, Kate, has returned from leave and is working a late shift that evening. She suggests spending time with Michael through the evening with the aim of getting to know him; she will also support him at bedtime.

Kate spends the evening in close proximity to Michael, often just sitting beside him on the settee watching television, offering him juice. Michael does not say much but doesn't appear to mind Kate's attention. Kate takes the opportunity to tell Michael that she always feels strange on her first evening back from holiday, as she catches up with everything and tries to get to know new children like Michael. It is part of the bedtime routine in the home that the younger children have the individual attention of a worker and Kate asks Michael if it is OK if she sees him up to bed. Michael nods that it will be OK. In the room Michael settles into bed and chooses a bedtime story, which Kate reads. At the end of the story Michael seems pretty relaxed.

Kate: "You seemed to enjoy that story, Michael."

Michael: "Yes."

Kate: "Now tell me what happens next – is it the floor or the bed?"

Michael (looking surprised, mumbles): "The floor."

Kate: "OK, is it the light or no light?"

Michael (again surprised, mumbles): "The light."

Kate: "Well, I am pleased you have been able to say what you want, because the other staff have told me that settling to bed has been really tough since you came. They don't understand why you prefer to sleep on the hard floor rather than the comfortable bed. Do you know the answer?"

Michael (shrugs his shoulders): "Dunno."

Kate: "I am usually a good guesser and you tell me if this is a good guess. I think you must have a very good reason for wanting to sleep on the floor and keep the light on, eh?"

Michael (looks bemused and shrugs again): "Dunno."

Kate: "When I was reading the bedtime story I thought you had a good imagination. Is that true?"

Michael: "Yes, sometimes."

Kate: "Well, let's pretend that your good imagination is with you and you imagine what a good reason might be for a boy like you wanting to keep his light on and sleep on the floor. Can you imagine a good reason?"

Michael: "Yes, sort of."

Kate: "Could you tell me what that would be?"

Michael: "Nightmares, maybe."

Kate: "That is a great reason why somebody might want to keep their light on and sleep on the floor. Is that the sort of reason why you would want to do the same?"

(Michael nods)

Kate: "Well, it sounds to me that you may have to sleep on the floor until you are sure those nightmares are away. We now need to think about ways that we can make sure you are comfortable on the floor and get a good night's sleep. Do you have any good ideas about that?"

The conversation continues for a short while and Michael agrees that maybe the mattress on the floor would be a good idea and also that he could have a night light that could be on so that his room is not completely dark. Kate tells Michael that she thinks these are great ideas and they move the mattress and find a night light. Kate says that it would be great if the nightmares could go away altogether but that might take a while. She ends by tucking Michael in and says if he wants, he can talk to her again about how the nightmares might go away altogether.

Introduction

Feeling safe and secure is a fundamental human need and one that provides an essential platform from which other needs and possibilities might be realised (Maslow, 1943; Kellmer–Pringle, 1975; Bowlby, 1988; Glasser, 1998; White, 2008). The idea of safety has in many ways become over-emphasised, yet it is poorly understood within dominant child protection or safeguarding discourses. Indeed, many of the practice perspectives that stem from child protection ways of thinking can get in the way of children feeling safe and having the confidence to use a developing sense of safety to start accessing a wider range of developmental needs and opportunities. Moreover, child protection predominantly identifies safety with systems and procedures rather than with emotions and relationships. These latter features of a sense of safety are what we seek to develop in this chapter, where we explore some practical meanings of safety – physical, emotional, relational and cultural.

Children entering residential child care often lack a sense of emotional safety and may have experienced disruption of their sense of belonging. This might be as a result of uncertainty and unpredictability in family care and relationships, but may be compounded through agency practices entailing multiple or serial placements. A primary task of residential care is to begin a process of helping children to feel safe. In this regard, their first encounters with carers can be crucial in determining how they might feel and subsequently respond to placement.

First encounters draw attention to one of the most important processes and tasks associated with child and youth care practice – initial engaging and relationship building with children and young people. How this first encounter is managed sets the tone for the developing relationship. One of the challenges carers face in meeting a new child invariably involves managing a child's anxieties, which may be projected through conformity, over-compliance, a couldn't-care-less attitude or aggression. Carers also have to manage their own anxieties and feelings of uncertainty. They may have heard something about a child's background and wonder how they might respond to one another. Reputations of challenging behaviour can be particularly anxiety provoking. Each participant in an encounter carries their own 'emotional baggage' and expectations that may influence the ease with which connections are made. While being aware of their own anxieties, carers need to tune in to ways of making contact with a young person. How agencies deal with admission and entry to the group is vitally important. This process needs to facilitate information gathering as well as to engage, reach out to and support a child or young person. How first encounters are managed communicates a great deal about the social climate of a child's new home, school or residence.

Routines, rhythms and rituals of daily living

Maier's 'The core of care' (1979) draws attention to the practices of daily living that help children and young people feel safe. Engaging in daily interactions – or relational exchanges – with children and young people forms the basis of their developing sense of safety. 'The core of care' introduces the terms 'routines, rhythms and rituals'. We all need some structure and routine in our lives – children and young people admitted to care perhaps more than most. Many are admitted at a point where their lives have lost any structure or meaning. They need to experience a sense of order and organisation in their lives that restores some coherence to the chaotic and disintegrated circumstances in which they have often been living; to experience a structure that is resilient enough to withstand their emotional chaos, while experiencing such structure as stable and credible (Kornerup, 2009). This is a prerequisite before they can begin to address some of the more specific difficulties that may have contributed to their admission to care and before they can be in a position to consider taking the next steps towards healing and growth. Experience tells us that children may initially resist our attempts to impose some order and organisation on their lives. It also tells us that most will come to accept and appreciate them. A sense of their lives gradually coming under more control happens, primarily, though the experience of nurturing everyday care and the presence of caring and suitably resilient adults.

Returning to Maier's terms, 'routine' refers to the structures of a place – that sense of what follows what in the course of a day. Thus, children should know what time they will be expected to get up in the mornings, what happens at mealtimes and other times of the day, through to what time they are required to go to bed. This provides them with a sense of predictability. Care must be taken to ensure that the routine doesn't become 'routinised' in the sense that it becomes inflexible and time slots inviolable. Maier (1979) cautions that a healthy sense of order doesn't come from a book of house rules but needs to grow out of the lived experience of those who live and work in a home. In this sense, Maier's idea of 'rhythm' perhaps captures what a healthy residential home might aspire towards. This is a state where order develops organically and where things happen because they become ingrained in the everyday life events of a home.

In every home or residence, each day follows particular rhythms around mealtimes, sleep, work or play times – and all of these require sensitive daily and weekly management (Fulcher, 2005). Rhythms of daily living may alter to accommodate different evening and weekend routines and activities. Set meals might be set aside, for instance, to accommodate a take-away or a barbecue. Weekly and monthly rhythms of care can be identified through an examination of school and recreational activities, shopping and laundry practices, television viewing, and so on. Monthly and seasonal rhythms of care are also associated with school, work and holiday periods.

To get to this stage requires a general agreement from young people and staff that the expectations that frame routines are reasonable and sensible. This allows a situation to develop where things happen because children and adults are 'in tune' with one another and there is an acceptance that 'this is the way things are done around here'. Appropriate 'rituals' of care can help bring about this level of acceptance. Essentially, rituals are those encounters between young people and staff that develop and have a particular meaning for those engaging in them. Thus, the particular ways we get young people up in the morning, the individualised ways we greet them through gestures or actions such as 'high fives', all contribute towards an experience of care that is personal rather than merely instrumental. Rituals speak of a personal connection. They oil the smooth running of a home. At another level, rituals may become apparent through particular religious or seasonal practices such as the way that festivals or celebrations like birthdays are dealt with, or even such practices as playing ball games in the garden during the summer months. The conscious use of these routines, rhythms and rituals of care is the starting point for allowing children and young people to feel safe.

Safety through relationships

While ideas of structure, routine, rhythm and ritual are important, they do not exist in their own right but only when enacted through relationships. As Kornerup suggests, 'when a child confronts structure, it is always in the guise of a person representing that structure. So, structure cannot be separated from contact' (2009: 50). This fact places carers at the heart of any sense of safety that a child might develop through exposure to the rhythms of everyday living. Any such sense is rooted in relational safety, within which the external structures, policies and procedures are only props that may help or, indeed, get in the way of a developing relationship. Being able to offer relational safety requires important qualities in a carer. Words and phrases such as 'authoritative' or 'firm but fair' can sound a bit old-fashioned in today's climate, but this is exactly how carers need to appear if they are to contain a child's anxiety. They may feel unsure and anxious below the surface but need to present themselves as being in control or at least being able to take control if required. While in the past personal authority might have begun and ended with a staff member's ability to maintain control, we now know that there is also merit in them leaving a way open to probe what might underlie behaviours. In this sense it is helpful for carers to acknowledge uncertainty and curiosity about what might be going on for a child or young person and to cede aspects of control over certain situations. An example of providing a sense of safety through the personal qualities of the carer might be illustrated in the following comment from a former children's home resident: 'There was a nun, who was the head nun of our children's home who was very, very fair, and kind, but not in a 'goody-goody' way – she was a just person, and she offered us protection' (David, in Cree and Davis, 2008: 87).

Some theoretical ideas relating to safety

Attachment

Attachment theory has returned to prominence in recent writing on residential child care (for example, Sharpe, 2006; Cameron and McGinn, 2008), to the extent that it has been adopted by many agencies as their underpinning theoretical model of practice. It offers a unique lens through which to understand children's experiences and behaviours and offers ideas as to how we might work with them in residential child care settings. The application of attachment theory to residential child care, however, should not be considered in an overly abstract or clinical sense but needs to make sense and be made sense of within the particular context of everyday living.

Specifically, attachment theory offers insights into how children and young people might experience a sense of safety and security. A central tenet in attachment theory is that of anxiety: basically, it suggests that we are all prey to a primitive sense of anxiety. Carers need to be able to manage a child's anxiety to prevent this from becoming self-destructive. In babies this happens when caregivers respond to an infant's distress by providing physical and emotional comfort. When a caregiver's response occurs with sensitivity and consistency, then children can form an attachment bond with him or her. If this bond is what Winnicott (1965) terms 'good enough', it allows infants to develop what attachment theorists call an internal working model of the world as benign and trustworthy. They learn to regulate their emotions and to explore their worlds, confident of the existence of a secure base to which they can return. 'Good enough' parenting figures provide what Winnicott (1965) calls a 'facilitating environment' – a stable physical and emotional environment where a child is safe, yet allowed sufficient space to grow and to build healthy trusting relationships that will provide the template for subsequent relationships.

The failure to provide such an environment in early childhood gives rise to anxieties and fears, some of which may be unconscious (Sharpe, 2006). Anglin (2002) identifies much of the behaviour presented by children in residential child care as being pain-based. Children seek to defend themselves against anxiety and emotional pain by employing a range of psychological defence mechanisms. They may 'project' onto others what is too difficult for them to hold inside. Unhappy children often express the fears and frustrations of their past by 'transferring' their emotional distress onto residential workers. In practice these behaviours may be described and experienced as aggression or acting out or anger management problems. Being confronted by expressions of a child's anxiety and anger can in turn arouse primitive anxieties in the worker, through a dynamic known as 'counter-transference'. Responses to children based upon counter-transference reactions can lead workers to react in a tit-for-tat manner, responding to aggression with counter-aggression and meeting anxiety with further anxiety. The task for workers in such situations is, like good parents, to try to understand why a child might be behaving in a particular way, to process their feelings and give them back to the child in a way that will reassure him or her (Sharpe, 2006).

Some caution is, however, required in the application of attachment and trauma-based approaches. In externalising their anxieties, children and young people are at the same time asking for these to be managed. Carers, within a psychodynamic model, cannot allow themselves to become overwhelmed by children's past experiences and resultant anxieties, but need to respond confidently and spontaneously in the here and now to children's behaviour. This is rarely straightforward; therapeutic relationships can be messy and may at times involve conflict between adults and children and both parties can make mistakes in such encounters. In this regard, Winnicott's notion of 'good enough' rather than ideal parenting is an important one.

Containment

Wilfred Bion's (1962) concept of 'containment' offers parallels with Winnicott's facilitating environment. This concept provides a way of understanding the process by which carers receive the projected, intolerable feelings of an infant, but modify and return them in such a way that these become tolerable; thus the caregiver is termed the 'container' and the infant is 'contained'. Early and repeated experiences of containment enable a child to manage emotions. By contrast, when experiences of containment are inadequate or significantly interrupted, children's cognitive and emotional development and their capacity to manage emotions are adversely affected (Steckley, 2010). Ward (1995) identifies the needs children have for both literal containment, in terms of basic care and the setting of boundaries, and metaphoric containment, which involves the worker soaking up a child's uncontainable feelings. Staff teams need to create and maintain cultures that are strong enough to withstand and contain children's anxieties and to give them experiences and tools that might help them establish healthy and intimate relationships in their adult lives. A primary aim of residential homes, therefore, should be to try and encourage and maintain containing relationships rather than to focus directly on issues of control. Effective control will only come about if children feel that their anxieties are suitably understood and contained.

Attachment to place: a sense of belonging

Attachment theory tends to be considered in the context of interpersonal relationships. Another important consideration, however, is attachment to place. This is central to children's development of a healthy identity, security and sense of belonging (Jack, 2010). Belonging can be defined as 'a sense of ease with oneself and one's surroundings' and involves 'a process of creating a sense of identification with one's social, relational and material surroundings' (May, 2011: 368). It thus includes a sense of place and a connected importance with others. Acquiring such a sense of place may hold particular significance for children in residential child care in situations where their life experiences have often been disrupted and insecure.

A sense of belonging grows alongside feelings of being valued by and attached to other individuals. This may involve other people with whom a young person lives, or peers in a neighbourhood or community: attachments formed from the young person's activities as a player in a football team, a band member, a participant in a theatre group or involvement with a particular culture and people through religious activities, performance or celebrations. A sense of belonging is fundamental to developing a sense of self-worth (Laursen, 2005). In residential child care a sense of belonging is nurtured through the everyday habits, practices and experiences of care (Garfat, 1998).

Belonging provides a secure physical and emotional base from which children and young people comfortably venture into their world, try new things, and successfully engage in new experiences. Belonging with others develops through a sense of identification with those particular others, and evolves as people do things together. Thus, doing things with young people is an important part of their development. Belonging is one of the most basic of human needs and without a sense of belonging a young person feels detached, disconnected and alone. This may leave them prone to seeking connections exclusively through their peer group or perhaps through involvement in particular subcultures or gangs (Centre for Social Justice, 2008).

Attachment to place grows in the course of daily living, through 'a large number of routine activities and everyday experiences' (Jack, 2010: 757). Drawing on psychoanalytic theory, Jack suggests that the way people think about places is 'incorporated into the self, creating internalized objects that serve as sources of security at times of stress or isolation' (2010: 757). At times of stress we all tend to think back to the comforts and security of home. The same is true for former residents of care homes. Letters sent back to staff of a Scottish approved school from former pupils who had been sent to the trenches during the First World War speak of fond memories of their time spent in the school as they were about to go 'over the top'. One of the respondents to an oral history project undertaken in a residential school said "I loved my time here. ... If I could turn the clock back I would come back here. ... I miss both staff and pupils." Another respondent noted that "the skills taught on Mr Hill's work parties stay with me to this day. Every time I drop a tree or split a log, his voice guides my hand" (Smith, 2008).

The development of a sense of belonging, therefore, needs to incorporate attachment relationships with particular individuals but also to take into account the meaning attached to place. For many children in care, attachment to place may be more important than attachments to individuals. It may involve relationships with a number of different individuals, some more significant than others, which come together in a memory of place.

Bearing in mind the importance of place in nurturing a sense of belonging might encourage carers to consider what kind of feelings, and ultimately what kind of memories, children and young people might have of place. The introduction of memory boxes in recent times, whereby children are encouraged to store mementos and keepsakes from various points in their lives, has become one way in which these connections might be maintained. Images, sounds and smells that reflect particular rhythms of caring are likely to be incorporated into how children and young people experience and remember a place. Flowers on the table, smells of fresh coffee or home baking, memories of sitting around chatting and laughing after a meal, the instructions given on how to carry out a particular task: these are all likely to evoke a particular sense of place.

Applying ideas of attachment and containment: Maier's 'core of care'

We have already referred to Henry Maier's 'core of care' (1979). This, we believe, offers a compelling conceptual framework through which to consider how a sense of relational safety and wellbeing can be developed through everyday living, and it is these ideas we now develop.

Component 1: bodily comfort

Bodily comfort is basic to personal care. This frequently involves activities that may be taken for granted. Throughout life, a sense of wellbeing and care is experienced when one's body feels secure and free from stress. Physical comfort is strengthened through the involvement of another person. It is this investment of personal energy in attending to personal comfort and physical safety that converts physical care into active caring. Consider the caring act of straightening out a young person's bed sheets so that she or he might sleep in greater comfort, or providing a hot water bottle on a cold night. Consider the act of sitting down on the floor with a child in order to afford him or her a more relaxed bodily posture and more convenient eye level. Maier claims that as a child's bodily comfort needs are met, so does he or she feel cared about and cared for.

A concern for physical comfort and security extends to the way we deal with a child or young person's personal space, both in their presence and during their absence. It is also significant that when children or young people move from one setting to another, they often require help in order to make the unfamiliar familiar. Transitional objects – a much-loved blanket or cushion, stuffed toy, photo or trinket – may serve as a link that helps transform a strange place into something more familiar. Familiarity then equates with a feeling of security.

Component 2: differences

Individual and personal differences contribute towards inherently different interactions between carers and children and young people. From birth, children are quite different in temperament, and such differences bring about a wide variety of interactions with, as well as from, their carers. A young person's daily interactions are shaped by native temperament as well as by differences in their personal histories, gender and social class. A child's temperament, interacting with their environment, shapes the quality of their interactions. Thus, rather than establishing standardised expectations of behaviour, it is far more productive for carers to align their responses to the unique characteristics of the child or young person living in their residence, thereby increasing the likelihood of achieving more effective and natural responses.

Some children and young people absorb rapidly what is going on around them: what Maier calls 'living radars'. While appearing to sit back and not be particularly involved, they are active 'stimulus scanners', picking up on all that happens around them. These are the children that can tell you all the gossip that is going down in a home. Other children seem only to find out about their world through bumping into it – these 'stimulus-bound' or 'go-go' children and young people enter immediately into whatever is happening within their reach. These are the children that demand a response from carers, usually one that is aimed at getting them to sit in one place long enough to be able to engage with them. Living radars and go-go children elicit and demand different responses from carers. Specifically, carers may need to remind themselves that the living radars are there and merit attention. This may need only minimal activity on the part of the carer: a raised eyebrow, a brush of the shoulders, an acknowledgement of shared knowledge and understanding of an event. Go-go children, on the other hand, require a more hands-on and active engagement. Knowing how best to tailor their responses according to the temperament of particular children is something that carers build up through the development of rhythmic interactions between the two parties.

Component 3: rhythmic interactions

Rhythmicity – the inclination to engage in rhythmic interactions with another – is a vital feature of human development; a hallmark of 'togetherness' in later life events, such as in group singing or dance, imaginative play, team sports or even sexual activity. Rhythmicity is an underlying force that brings children or young people together with caring adults where they must somehow find their joint rhythms. This might be thought of in terms of a table tennis ball being bounced from one side of a table to the other – a certain rhythm emerges. Rhythms can similarly emerge in human interactions; elements of human behaviour require the blending together of an individual's internal bio-rhythms with rhythmic demands in the new environment in which they live. It is this subtle rhythmic involvement that determines the quality and, possibly, the overall direction an interaction takes. Interpersonal rituals such as handshakes or ruffling of hair are social counterparts to psychological rhythmicity. Through such rituals of encounter, people experience a sense of connection and togetherness. Discussion of rhythmicity might fit with the idea of 'mind-mindedness', whereby parents become able to tune into and treat their children as individuals with minds rather than merely entities with needs to be met (Petrie et al, 2006). Recognising one another as thinking, feeling subjects might allow for the development of appropriate rhythmic responses.

Component 4: predictability

The capacity to predict something is a measure of knowing. This cognitive dimension of knowing – of predictability that I can do that again and again – goes hand in hand with a child or young person's feelings of certainty or sense of assurance. Predictability is thus an essential ingredient of effective learning. To know what might happen in the immediate future lends a sense of order and power, as well as a tremendous feeling of security. Through a developing sense of predictability about what happens in certain circumstances, a child or young person feels safe and secure enough to keep returning to further learning opportunities with particular people, trusting that the outcomes are predictably manageable, even helpful. Interpersonally, the development of rhythmicity might be likened to learning new dance steps. It is tentative and a bit uncertain as dancing partners become attuned to one another. The stepping in and stepping out again that is part of this process seems to reflect what goes on in the development of new relationships, until the different partners become increasingly comfortable and sure of one another's next steps; these become predictable. The long-term effects of predictability (or knowing what will happen next) are very influential, especially when combined with dependability, the emotional dimension of trust.

Component 5: dependability

Dependency flows from predictability. Within some social work circles that place high value on qualities of independence and empowerment, ideas of dependency can be frowned upon. Yet qualities of independence and empowerment are at times overemphasised in care contexts. Dependency is natural and desirable, and an essential feature of caring for children and young people! Paradoxically, it is only through the experience of healthy dependency that children can, in time, move towards meaningful independence. Attempts to minimise dependency in order to promote independence are thus ill conceived. There can be a focus in some children's homes on seeking to prepare children for independence by placing them in self-catering flats, by expecting them to assume budgetary responsibility and by teaching them some instrumental skills deemed to be helpful for living alone. Such initiatives are unlikely to be successful on their own. Knowing how to boil an egg or wire a plug is of limited use when young people don't feel emotionally able to live alone. They only achieve this level of independence once they have experienced a strong and safe experience of dependency.

As children or young people come to know and to predict their experiences with others, so they grow to depend upon these people. It feels good to depend on someone else. It assures the child or young person that they are not alone and that they can depend or rely upon someone for support. The feeling of dependence creates attachment, and having attachments – and feeling dependence and depended upon – feels good for both carer and young person. Bronfenbrenner (1979) argues that every child needs at least one person who is really crazy about him or her. When a child or young person feels that someone cares for them and their wellbeing, that someone is crazy about them and really believes in them, they start to feel better about themselves in the immediate setting, and begin to feel hopeful about future relationship opportunities with other important people in their lives. When people experience secure dependence between one another they can function more independently, as they feel assured of mutual attachment. Secure dependence stimulates independence and ultimately freedom to enter into new dependency relationships; thence healthy care giving relationships.

Component 6: personalised behavioural training

Social capabilities and competencies rest upon personal attachments. Thus far there have been no references to discipline or training in self-management and manners. Yet these questions of rules and structure are central concerns of carers. Some structure, some house rules are essential. These, however, should be kept to a minimum – perhaps around bedtimes, expectations of school attendance and general respect for the environment and for fellow residents and staff. Children and young people respond to and learn most readily from those with whom they have a relationship, and who have special meaning for them. They turn to the people who can be counted upon; namely, those they perceive as being with them or on their side. Older siblings and peers, perhaps a few steps ahead in their development, often become role models. Emond's (2004) study of resident group functioning in children's homes confirms that fellow residents do indeed perform important roles in offering a sense of support to their peers. The group needs to be recognised for its potential to promote healthy norms around questions of safety, rather than being conceived of in negative terms or implicated in bullying. These role models can have equal status, or even greater importance to young people than their designated carers. The most potent behavioural training goes hand in hand with a sense of reciprocal closeness and attachment. When children or young people and caring adults have a relationship characterised by rhythmicity, effective social training and more complicated socialisation efforts actually begin. Nurturing self-management and enriching a child or young person's behavioural repertoires are closely linked to quality relationships with carers.

Component 7: care for the caregiver(s)

Maier's seventh component of care changes tack somewhat. Recognising that if one wishes to support children's upbringing, a good starting point is to provide suitable care and support to parents, Maier extends this argument to incorporate care for what might be termed, nowadays, corporate parents. Maier (1979) notes that caregivers are enriched or limited as agents of care according to the care they receive. There is, he argues, a direct connection between the quality of care received by the caregiver and the quality of care the caregiver is able to offer to young people. So, in helping children and young people feel safe, carers too need to feel suitably safe and supported. Within managerial cultures it might be argued that such support ought to be available through supervision. A problem with this is that within those self-same cultures the primary focus of much supervision has become one of accountability. This can make staff feel less sure, more vulnerable and afraid to admit to anxieties or uncertainty. Supervision in residential child care needs to develop to become congruent with the task of caring for children and young people. It needs to be an ongoing experience of support, offered primarily within a lifespace context, and to serve the function of containing carers' anxieties so that they might perform a similar task in respect of those for whom they care. Questions about leadership and leadership style, and about the confidence that staff members have in a leader's ability to soak up anxiety – from internal and external sources – to make them feel safe, are fundamental to this process.

Care for the caregiver(s) extends, however, beyond what happens in a residential care setting to include wider organisational climates. Maier (1985) notes the inherent strains involved in attempting to provide primary care in secondary settings where internal and wider organisational goals lack congruence. Carers need to feel that they are 'held in mind' by the organisation for which they work (Rose, 2010) and that their anxieties can be contained within the organisational context (Steckley, 2010). Cultures in which carers are afraid of the organisational response to mistakes or to possible allegations made against them are not conducive to the provision of caring care.

Family and extended family rhythms

In spite of what many professionals may wish or think, children and young people in care are still likely to resume contact and maintain involvement with family and extended family members while in and after leaving care (Fanshel et al, 1990). Children and young people have a strong sense of belonging to family, which is central to any secure sense of who they are. The point of admission to care can be a stressful one for children and young people and for their families. Tensions may be apparent and feelings raw. However, once children have settled into a new placement and some space has been put between the high emotions that might have been around at the point of admission, placement in residential care can provide an opportunity to develop stability and to facilitate improved family contact and relationships (Smith et al, 2004). It may be helpful, therefore, to identify kinship networks that help to give children and young people their social and cultural identities and to engage proactively with these (Burford and Casson, 1989).

Cultural and spiritual rhythms of caring

Cultural rituals of encounter and exchange are commonly overlooked in the delivery of social work and child and youth services (Fulcher, 1998). A sense of cultural safety is important for children and young people in residential care. Images, sounds and smells spring instantly to mind that reflect cultural and spiritual rhythms of caring, whether operating in a family or foster home, boarding school, group home or residential institution (Ramsden, 1997; Te Whaiti et al, 1997). Cultural safety involves the state of being in which a child or young person experiences that their personal wellbeing, as well as their social and cultural frames of reference, are acknowledged – even when not fully understood by carers. Cultural safety requires that each child or young person has reason for feeling hopeful that her or his needs will be attended to, in terms that she or he will understand. It means that family members and kin folk are accorded dignity and respect (Ramsden, 1997), and are actively encouraged to participate in decision making with service providers about the futures of their child(ren). Such respect needs to be shown – even, and perhaps particularly – to families who may, at one level, be thought to be unhelpful to their children as a result of particular lifestyles.

Summary

We have identified the foundational role of a sense of safety for children as a requirement in its own right but also as a basis for growth and development in other areas of life. Helping children and young people feel safe and secure needs to be considered beyond the realm of child protection procedures and what might be called safe caring practices. A sense of safety first and foremost stems from appropriate relationships. The development of relational trust is a fundamental ingredient of healing. This enables children and young people in care to develop a sense of belonging in a world that is safe and secure.

Building from Maier's (1979) arguments about the 'core of care', attention has focused on rhythms of daily living that help children and young people learn predictability and dependability. Predictability and dependability are the foundations for emotional security and trust. Consistency in how we behave with individual children or young people is also important if carers are to offer them opportunities to experience a secure place and a social world that is more predictable than that which they may have experienced previously. In care, young people can be offered opportunities to develop a sense of belonging in peer and adult relationships, especially when carers welcome young people and enable them to relax and be comfortable. Relationships flourish when a child or young person's basic wants and needs are met in a caring and nurturing manner with others.

Returning to the scenario

Essentially, Kate respected Michael's 'space' and paced her engagement with him. She shared her own anxiety about getting to know new children. She checked throughout the evening, by her proximity and attentiveness, that he was comfortable with her presence and her wish to get alongside him. The acceptance of the bedtime story and the implicit intimacy gave her permission to investigate his anxiety about sleep and darkness in a gentle and normalising way. Depending on the particular child and staff member, appropriate touch by means of a hug or other physical expression of reassurance might be helpful in such situations (Petrie et al, 2006).

Kate's containment of her own anxiety that Michael might react aggressively, as he had done to others, helped them reach a workable solution that ensured his comfort and safety, and she did not set up as a potential conflict by falling back on rigid house rules such as 'You must sleep in the bed with the light out'. She was willing to stay in tune with the child's expressed needs rather than rigid enforcement of routine and policies. The worker was confident enough to adjust expectations, yet she acknowledged that there would be a time when he would not feel the 'need' to sleep on the floor and in the dark.

Thoughts for practice

Think about how first encounters with newly arrived residents are managed. These encounters need to be paced so as to strike a balance between being experienced as too impersonal or remote and, conversely, feeling too superficially friendly and possibly uncomfortable within the context of a new relationship. Carers need to take their cue from children as to how close these initial encounters ought to be, taking into account individual temperament.

For children and young people who have been in a residence for a while, consider what rituals of encounter – such as how they are awakened in the mornings or how they are greeted – fit with individual temperament and might contribute or otherwise to a feeling of safety.

Bodily comfort and hence a feeling of safety can be helped by attending to practical matters such as offering an extra blanket or pillow, a hot water bottle, juice, biscuits, fruit, extension leads, light bulbs, coat hangers, a waste basket, tissues. Finding out about individual likes and dislikes – such as how someone takes their tea or what their favourite meal is – likewise contributes to a sense of feeling safe and cared for.

In staff teams it may be helpful to identify, explore and then actively nurture rhythms of daily life in the home – around school, family and individual mealtimes, chores and responsibilities, TV, homework, recreation activities, leisure pursuits and spiritual life as appropriate – and think about how these might encourage or detract from children feeling cared for. It may pay dividends to think about and develop youth-friendly as well as centre-friendly rituals (for example, high fives, special handshakes, friendly banter or rewards for high achievement) and to consider what functions these may serve in 'oiling' relationships.

Similarly, it is worth paying attention to the immediate environment to consider what a child or young person might experience and hence remember their time in a home – what smells, sounds, images will contribute to their sense of place? Are there pictures on the wall, smells of home baking, cushions on chairs, all of which small things evoke memories of feeling cared for. Consider the use of memory boxes for children – a designated container or place where personal mementos, treasures and trivia can be stored in a safe manner – and discuss with children what items they might have that they want to store there.

Get into the habit of spending time together with a child or young person to review the events of the day and talk about what is coming up tomorrow and during the rest of the week, in order to establish a sense of predictability. Actively explore ways in which children or young people living in your home, school or centre might meet other family or extended family members, family friends, or schoolmates. For example, evenings where children or young people might invite family members for a meal that they cook can help children feel that their families are accepted by their care setting.

Further reading

Henry Maier's (1979) 'The core of care' is well worth a read and is available on CYC-Net:

www.cyc-net.org/CYR101C/pdf/maier-ingredients.pdf

Two articles that discuss psychodynamic perspectives are:

Sharpe, C. (2006) 'Residential child care and the psychodynamic approach: is it time to try again?', *Scottish Journal of Residential Child Care*, vol 5, no 1, pp 46–56.

Steckley, L. (2012) 'Touch, physical restraint and therapeutic containment in residential child care', *British Journal of Social Work*, vol 42, no 3, pp 537–55.

Nurtured: a sense of care

3

Scenario

Tony is 13 and has been living in one of the cottage units in a residential school for six months where he is settled and doing very well. His early years were characterised by frequent spells of being looked after in short-term foster placements due to his family's chaotic lifestyle and their poor physical and emotional care of him. Tony seems to have survived his early years' experiences very well. He remains close to his parents, whom he sees regularly. He realises, though, that they cannot provide the stability he requires and he has now got used to this.

Tony is intelligent, sporty and has some status in his peer group. He is well liked by other children. He can, however, appear uninterested and moody, and when in such a state can be stubborn and confrontational with children and staff. Increasingly, though, he displays an engaging side to his character and has a well-developed sense of humour. He enjoys the 'banter' that goes on between the adults in the staff group. For their part, the staff have realised that humour can be a successful strategy at those times when Tony is getting agitated.

Early one morning, Tony arrives in the administration office of the school with Adam, one of the young care workers. They have come to collect money for a shopping trip to town so that Tony can get some new clothes. Ian, one of the school's senior managers, is in the office. Tony looks like he has just got out of bed; his blond hair is unkempt and he still has sleep in his eyes. He has clearly not had a shower. He has a bit of a frown on his face and his mood seems a bit flat. Ian is not impressed by Tony's appearance but Adam seems oblivious to it.

Ian (in a loud and playful tone): "My goodness you guys are up early! Wait – no I get it – you didn't go to bed last night, you were so desperate to get out shopping today. Is that right, Adam? You kept Tony awake all night so that you could go early to the shops?"

Before Adam gets a chance to answer Ian gets up and walks over to Tony who now has a grin on his face.

Ian (direct to Tony): "Tony, is that true that Adam didn't let you get to sleep last night? Eh? Is it true?" (He playfully tussles Tony's unkempt hair.)

Tony starts to laugh as Adam looks on, beginning to realise that Ian has a point to make but also appreciating the humour of Ian's approach.

Tony: "No."

Ian: "No? What do you mean, 'no'? If you haven't been up all night how come you don't look your normal handsome self? Your hair hasn't been combed, there is sleep in your eyes and I can't smell that expensive shower gel that you normally wear. Wait! Don't answer – I think I know what has happened."

Ian (turning to Adam and continuing in an exaggeratedly playful tone): "So what are you guys on the staff being paid for, eh? You can't be bothered to make sure Tony is looking his best before he meets his public in town today – more interested in your own style and fancy haircut, eh? Tony, somebody could be in deep trouble here! Have you any sympathy for him?"

Tony and Adam are now laughing at Ian's 'over the top' performance.

Tony: "Not really."

Ian (to Tony): "So you think Adam deserves to get into trouble for this?"

Tony (laughing): "Yes, sack him."

Ian: "Well, I'll think about sacking him. In the meantime I suggest you nip back to the cottage with him and have a quick wash, spray yourself with smelly stuff and put a comb through your hair. When you come back I'll make a decision about sacking Adam and have your money ready."

Tony and Adam leave the office with Adam giving Tony a (mock) hard time for getting him into trouble. Tony is laughing and teasing Adam that he has got him sacked.

Introduction

This chapter is about upbringing and related concepts of nurture, child rearing, or just plain care or care giving. In using these terms we are talking about the broad range of practices that promote children's overall development. In that sense, each chapter in this book might, rightly, be argued to fit within a broad conception of upbringing. In this chapter we focus on some of the nurturing activities of everyday life, which come together to contribute to an overall sense of care. A sense of care involves 'relations of dependence and independence, relations of giving and receiving' (Lynch et al, 2009: 49). Being and feeling cared for is a prerequisite for human development. The forms of social engagement that emerge from caring relations 'are frequently what brings meaning, warmth and joy to life' (Lynch et al, 2009: 1). In residential settings, care is not offered and received merely between those employed to care and those cared for, but within a wider matrix of care. Care giving practices are also apparent in the daily lives and interactions which are evident within groups of residents: 'Such care-giving and receiving requires and results from human interdependence, from conceptualizing persons as relational rather than autonomous' (Emond, 2010: 75).

We noted in Chapter One how ideas of care have become marginalised in social work, being associated with a sense of dependency by a profession that identifies the promotion of autonomy and independence as central objectives. Social work courses exhort students to identify what the social work task is in any situation. Making sure that children brush their teeth and have clean socks is not, generally, considered to be social work. Indeed, social work students can struggle even to think of residential care placements as providing them with the kind of opportunities to demonstrate their social work competence. Yet tasks to do with socks and teeth cleaning are central to residential child care. Expressions of care are often manifest in the little things of everyday life (Costa and Walter, 2006): the touch, the gesture, the laundered bedsheets, the bunch of flowers on the kitchen table. Redl and Wineman talk about the need for 'a home that smiles, props which invite, space which allows' (1957: 6). Conversely, the institutional trappings – such as the fire exit or no smoking signs or the ubiquitous visitor book – that are features of many care homes speak of a very different type of care experience.

Although the term 'care' features in the title, *Residential child care*, just what this means is rarely addressed, but needs to be. Care is not the primarily technical/rational task it has become in dominant professional and political ways of thinking. It is, in essence, a moral and practical endeavour (Moss and Petrie, 2002). It is not easily measured and its outcomes are far from certain or predictable. Caring relationships '... are predicated on an expressive rather than instrumental relationship to others (based on) trust, commitment over time and a degree of predictability' (Brannen and Moss, 2003).

In order for care to become an expressive rather than merely an instrumental activity, it is necessary for physical care to be transformed into caring care. This happens when the 'self' of the carer becomes central to the experience of care. Such occasions are 'our whispered moments of glory;

our Camelots' (Maier, 1979). To illustrate this point we might think about how we get children up in the morning. We could stand outside their room and knock on their door, shouting at them to get up, or we could go into their room, open their curtains and ruffle their hair. The former approach might achieve its aim of ensuring that a child or young person gets up; the latter might speak of this transformation of physical care into caring care. On the other hand, some children may only need and prefer a less intimate wake up call. The true expression of personalised care is a carer's ability to tune into what is right for particular children.

Care ethics

The growing literature around care ethics provides a helpful body of theory within which to think about care as a fundamentally moral and practical activity enacted through everyday relational encounters. Care ethics are emerging as an important strand of ethical thinking with particular relevance to residential child care (Steckley and Smith, 2011). They stem from the work of Carol Gilligan (1993), who proposes that men and women adopt different approaches to moral thinking: a male voice speaking of rules and principles and foregrounding a justice orientation; the female voice highlighting qualities of compassion and intuition – what Gilligan terms a care voice. For this reason, care ethics are often thought of as feminist ethics. The association of justice and care voices with men and women respectively has moved on since Gilligan's early work, and the voices are now considered more as general orientations to moral thinking rather than necessarily being linked to a particular gender.

Writers on care ethics would suggest that the dominant approach to public care is a justice one, based around rights and principles. Care ethics, on the other hand, emphasise responsibilities and relationships instead of rules and rights, being bound to concrete situations rather than being abstract and formal (Sevenhuijsen, 1998). Tronto, likewise, identifies care as 'a practice, rather than a set of rules or principles. ... It involves both particular acts of caring and a "general habit of mind" to care' (1994: 126–7). Anyone who has spent much time in residential child care settings – and, more importantly, children who have grown up in such settings – can identify those workers who demonstrate a general habit of mind to care and, indeed, those who do not.

According to Held, 'a caring person not only has the appropriate motivations in responding to others or in providing care but also participates adeptly in effective practices of care' (2006: 4). The importance of participating in acts or practices of care may go some way towards distinguishing between the respective roles of direct care workers and social workers. In this respect,

Noddings (1984; 2002a) differentiates between 'caring about' and 'caring for'. 'Caring about' involves having a view or taking a stance on an issue; it does not require the provision of direct care but reflects a general predisposition to see that children are well treated. But 'caring about' isn't enough on its own. One can profess to care about something without getting one's hands dirty in the messy business of 'caring for'. One can make a point, hand over a donation and walk away. Noddings (1984) suggests that 'caring about' can involve a certain benign neglect; it is empty if it does not result in caring relations. Residential child care, by contrast, requires that workers are primarily called to 'care for' children and young people. They work at the level of the face-to-face encounter, engaging in everyday practices of care such as getting children up in the mornings, encouraging their personal hygiene, engaging in a range of social and recreational activities with them and ensuring appropriate behaviours and relationships within the group. Carers are also confronted with the intensity of children's emotions and get involved in the messy and ambiguous spaces around intimacy and boundaries. An inevitable messiness and ambiguity enters the fray when workers become involved in 'caring for' (Steckley and Smith, 2011).

In respect of residential child care, in fact, it may be that merely 'caring about' can get in the way of 'caring for'. When we are only concerned to 'care about' children we can construct them as abstractions – we don't need to confront them in the messiness and rawness of the face-to-face encounter.

The way that social welfare has become professionalised tends to privilege 'caring about'. Those who 'care about' have considerably more status that those who 'care for'; in the same way, social workers have far more clout than residential care workers. Yet, ironically, it is social workers who are vested with expertise in care, an area in which many of them may have little direct experience. As a result, care plans can demonstrate a 'paint by numbers' approach to caring, which strips it of its richness and ambiguity. Of course we need to 'care about' and assert a worldview that speaks of our hopes for children and young people. But 'caring about' only achieves proper meaning and proper perspective when we are prepared to get our hands dirty in the task of 'caring for'.

Fisher and Tronto (1990) and Tronto (1994) extend understandings of care beyond just care giving to include the category of care receiving. This requires that we think about care, not as a one-way dynamic where care is 'done to' the cared for by the one caring, but as a reciprocal relationship. It can be assumed within current policy that residential care workers are mere dispensers of care. This reinforces a view of young people as largely passive recipients of care, thus denying their active involvement in caring relationships and their agency in shaping their own experience of care. An appreciation of care as reciprocal brings with it an awareness of the complex psychodynamic processes that emerge within particular relationships, and requires carers to consider that what might work in one situation between a particular child and a particular worker might not in another. Practice needs to be grounded in the context and nature of particular relationships.

Love and right relationships

Care is enacted through relationships, and the relationships between carers and young people are the primary means through which opportunities for healing, development and flourishing are provided. Noddings cites Uri Bronfenbrenner's oft-quoted assertion that a child needs 'the enduring, irrational involvement of one or more adults in care and joint activity … Somebody has to be crazy about that kid' (cited in Noddings, 2002a: 25). When an adult is crazy about a kid and that kid knows it, children can, in Noddings' terms, 'glow and grow'.

Being crazy about a kid you work with, talks of strong emotions, emotions that might take us in the direction of considering that carers might even love those they care for.

Admitting to being crazy about a kid or that you might experience feelings that might tend towards what we might think of as loving, has not been a good idea in the risk averse and child protection dominated climates that have enveloped residential child care in recent years, where fear rather than love has been the dominant emotion. (Smith, 2008)

The difficulty we have in talking about love in a professional context is philosophically problematic. Philosophers identify a capacity, and indeed a calling, within human nature to reach out to 'the other'. John MacMurray (2004), for instance, claims that the capacity to love objectively is what makes us people: we become so through our relationships with others. Care is not possible, according to MacMurray, in terms of duty and obligation but must emerge as an ethic of love.

There are some signs that things are changing, to the extent that even policy documents are starting to identify the importance of love in the care of looked after children. Guidance from the Social Care Institute of Excellence and the National Institute for Clinical Excellence notes that love and affection are essential but are often lacking in the lives of children in care, and that this has a significant impact on their emotional wellbeing and, for some, a lasting impact on their future prospects. The guidance concludes by identifying a 'child's need to be loved and nurtured [as] fundamental to achieving long-term physical, mental and emotional wellbeing' (SCIE–NICE 2011: 9). The literature on child care, similarly, is increasingly talking of love (for example, White, 2008). Garfat and Fulcher (2011) go even further and identify love as one of the characteristics of a child and youth care approach to practice.

Talk of love in a professional context is not that of a 'fluffy', feel-good sort of love; nor is it a romantic love. It is bound up with the very notion of care. Lynch et al (2009) talk interchangeably of love, care and solidarity. Loving relationships are rarely bland. Nor are they necessarily consensual and cosy but can be fraught and conflictual, and can, at times, involve strong negative feelings. But, if they are characterised by a belief that the relationship will endure beyond the difficult episodes, then they will be worked through and will come to cement the relational bond. It is the same with professional relationships:

> There are times that we need to fall out with those we work with, but we need to have the courage to do this at a relational level rather than hiding behind legislation and systems to do so and then point them towards some formal complaints system when they aren't happy with what we've done. (Smith, 2011a: 191)

White asserts that love grows in the woof and warp of everyday living, in 'the daily round and common task; the regular encounters, greetings and farewells, shared experiences …' (2008: 206) – a lifespace approach. The intimacy of such settings and the encounters that take place within them makes the growth of strong relationships that might rightly be considered loving almost inevitable. The love that might emerge out of this daily round is not the kind of outcome that policy makers may talk about and want to measure, but it is the kind of growth that emerges, slowly and unpredictably, out of the experience of human connection and relationship. But that relationship needs to be White's (2008) idea of right relationship, governed by the right intentions and competent action.

The emergence of right relationships in a lifespace context draws attention to the small things in daily living – the reciprocal, relational exchanges that go back and forth between workers and young people. A good example of this might be provided in the significance of a cup of tea.

> As many residential workers will recognise, one sugar or two, milky or weak: knowing how someone likes her tea is a powerful symbol of knowing and caring about her; sharing a cup, a medium for being in relationship together; correctly preparing it for another, a gesture to express the far too difficult words 'I'm sorry' or 'I care'. (Steckley and Smith, 2011:187)

The development of right or loving relationships demands a very different take on what has come to be considered 'professional'. In residential child care it used to be considered inevitable and valuable that children and adults were able to relate to one another as 'whole' people, in relationships not overly circumscribed by formalised roles (Beedell, 1970). Current dominant views of the 'professional' emphasise distance and objectivity in relationships (Meagher and Parton, 2004), a separation of emotions from actions; this is often about self-preservation, ensuring that carers don't do anything that might result in an allegation being made against them. It results in a distorted view of professionalism, which actually gets in the way of carers maximising any developmental purpose they might fulfil in the lives of children.

This separation of personal and professional selves is not without a purpose. It provides a defence against the strong emotions elicited by face-to-face contact with another. To hide behind a notion of professionalism can be handy when confronted with other people's pain, distress, anger or indeed attraction (Menzies Lyth, 1960). But there is a problem with this. The assumption that we can separate off our emotional from our rational – our personal from our professional selves – is increasingly difficult to sustain. Again, looking to MacMurray (2004), we are advised that our actions are motivated by our emotions as much as our intellect; we are feeling as well as thinking beings. In this sense, the central social pedagogical premise of carers employing 'head, heart and hands' in their work is a useful one to hold on to. Caring is intellectual, practical and emotional, and each of these dimensions interacts to influence the nature and quality of care offered and experienced.

Another helpful social pedagogical concept is that of the three Ps: the private, the personal and the professional (for example, Bengtsson et al, 2008). In a UK context we can be conditioned to construct relationships as either personal or professional and never to muddy the water between them. The idea of the third P introduces the private to this equation. It is only this private dimension that is kept hidden from those we work with. The personal and professional are seen as necessarily coming together within the 'self in action' task that is care giving. It is when we can bring our personal selves into caring relationships in a professional context that we can enter into such relationships with appropriate authenticity and spontaneity.

Touch

One of the most obvious and most powerful ways to express care is through physical touch. Touch is critical to proper human development, particularly in childhood; it is linked to physical, emotional and cognitive development, as well as the more specific areas of attachment, self-esteem and the ability to manage stress (Steckley, 2011). When working with challenging behaviour, touch can also reassure and defuse aggression in some young people (Steckley, 2011). Touch is an inevitable feature of lifespace work. Children bump into adults, deliberately or otherwise; they jump on one another and on adults and they initiate physical contact in a whole host of ways and for a whole host of reasons — looking for comfort at times of distress, affirmation of achievements or just a sense of connection with another human being.

Despite the benefits and the inevitability of touch in residential child care, assumptions that derive from child protection ways of thinking have infiltrated the sector and have become so embedded in policy and practice cultures that they can seem taken for granted. Thus, policies — and if not policies then deeply ingrained practice cultures — can lead workers to believe that they should not be involved in the physical touch of children or that they should not engage in activities such as horseplay with them. Such cultures can lead to strategies among staff where the primary impulse is to keep themselves rather than children safe (Horwarth, 2000). What used to be considered seemingly natural forms of interaction between adults and children have, within a wider climate of moral panic about touching children (Piper and Stronach, 2008), become regarded with suspicion to the point of being banned or narrowly prescribed in some residential child care settings (Steckley, 2011).

The climate that has emerged in relation to touching children in professional settings leads Kent (1997) in his *Children's safeguards review* to state that 'if child protection is the driving force (behind policy and practice developments) rather than child care, we may create a safe climate that is also a sterile climate'. He goes on to say: 'I have been saddened to hear of quite recent incidents of physical and sexual abuse. I have also been troubled to find that some carers in homes, schools or foster homes are now frightened to put an arm round any child' (1997: 4). In such situations we replace one tyranny — that of abuse — with another — a tyranny of blandness (McWilliam, 2000).

The uncertainty that surrounds touch practices in residential child care has wider ramifications; it percolates adult–child relationships more generally. Once touch stops being relaxed, spontaneous, or primarily concerned with responding to the needs of the child, it comes to be regarded as a self-conscious, negative act, controlled more by fear than a commitment to caring (Piper and Stronach, 2008). Carers become tentative and self-conscious in touching children who, in turn, pick up the adult's discomfort and potentially misinterpret it. Understandings of touch in such climates can become distorted; Steckley (2011), for instance, suggests that restraint might be used by children as a maladaptive means of achieving the kind of physical touch that they crave but that is denied them within current practice cultures.

In critiquing the climate that has grown up around touch we do not advocate that residential homes and schools become overtly or overly tactile places. Touch, when working with some children, can be a sensitive area of practice. Some may have particularly pronounced touch-related needs, due to previous experiences of neglect. Some may have experienced abusive or otherwise transgressive forms of touch, making it more difficult for them to initiate and accept being touched. Alternatively, they may be indiscriminate in seeking or initiating physical contact. Running alongside children's different experiences of touch, carers will have similarly different senses of what they are comfortable with. For those who are not naturally tactile, attempting to be so might be experienced as uncomfortable for both themselves and children.

As ever, the kind of relationships that exist between adults and children will be central to the way touch is used and experienced. Within trusting relationships touch is unlikely to be a sensitive issue. Skilful atunement and confidence are required for a carer to know how best to manage questions of who and when to touch. Prescriptive approaches fail to address the complexity of relationships, the particulars of a situation, and the individual needs of a child. Policies should not substitute for professional judgement in such complex practice arenas.

Food

In Chapter Two we considered Maier's (1979) 'The core of care' and identified within this the need for bodily comfort. An obvious prerequisite of feeling comfortable is feeling well fed. An appreciation of the importance of food and the rituals that surround it is one of the central features of residential child care. It is also one of the least explored. At a policy level, food seems to be dealt with in a primarily instrumental manner, surrounded by official rules and regulations that prevent carers from making children a sandwich without having first completed a food hygiene course. When it does get round to offering guidance on food, policy seems to struggle to move beyond healthy lifestyle exhortations to provide children and young people with five portions of fruit and vegetables a day – an aspiration with which many staff members are likely to struggle. This is a limited and limiting understanding of the role that food places in human life and culture. One might be forgiven for forgetting that eating might actually be a pleasurable experience and food consumption an enjoyable social ritual.

We have to go back to some of the pre-social work literature to find food being accorded its rightful place at the heart of thinking about care. Burmeister, for instance, notes that 'To be fed well and lovingly is one of the basic needs of all children, and the need is much greater for those who have not had continuous care in their homes' (1960: 38). Camphill schools, which have their origins in Aberdeenshire and are now a worldwide movement, appreciate this connection between food and love. Costa and Walter note that 'One of the keys to tasty food in Camphill is that magic spice called "love"' (2006: 40). They suggest that, when cooking, one should think of each person one is cooking for – their likes, dislikes and peculiarities – and that the end result of this process will be a meal that satisfies everyone.

It is only recently that research (Punch et al, 2009) has cast some light on the complex place that food has in residential child care and offers support to Burmeister's and Costa and Walter's claims. Interestingly, this research identifies the failure of current social work discourse to accord proper attention to the importance of food, noting that it can be difficult for carers 'to step back and look at the significance of small acts in relation to "the bigger picture" given the demands and responsibilities that [they] are required to meet' (Punch et al, 2009: 1). This bigger picture is the demands of care planning and paperwork and what are seen to be the 'professional' aspects of the job. Against this backdrop, the everydayness of food can mask its centrality in group living. Food is not just about physical sustenance but has symbolic significance as a means through which relationships can be established and developed. It is 'a medium through which connections with a place and people can be made. ... It can communicate recognition, acceptance or the claiming of a person or place through its link to personal needs' (Punch et al, 2009: 18). Carers, thus, can convey strong messages of acceptance and recognition through the way that they handle seemingly routine experiences such as the provision and consumption of food.

Mealtimes were identified by respondents to the Punch et al research as an important place for children to learn about behaviour, to acquire skills and to feel connected to one another and to their carers. They offer a real sense of belonging and closeness, offering opportunities to repair poor experiences and to relearn ways to socialise and make relationships. Hanging on at the dinner table after a meal is finished to continue chat and banter can be one of the most affirming and memorable experiences of a child's time in care.

While mealtimes hold out this possibility to be at the heart of a sense of nurture, they can also be fraught affairs. Whether they are or not is likely to depend on the wider culture and also the specific culture that has grown up around the importance of meals and mealtime in any particular setting. In Camphill schools, for instance, great attention is paid to the growing, sourcing and preparation of food. Rituals such as holding hands and singing grace before and after meals, as well as affirming a spiritual dimension to the schools' philosophy, play an important symbolic and practical role in marking the beginning and end of mealtimes. Such rituals have fallen out of practice in more mainstream settings, where they are considered institutional, possibly even religiously divisive or just too difficult to maintain. Mealtimes without appropriate rituals – and without appropriate understanding of their significance in the life of a home – stop being part of the community life and become potential flashpoints to get over and done with as quickly as possible.

Regulatory approaches to food in care settings seem to emphasise opportunities for children to participate in the process of menu planning, shopping and food preparation. These were not the kind of things identified by the young people in the Punch et al research as being particularly important. Some found these difficult or 'pointless'. What seemed to be more important was a sense of feeling cared for through the connections and relationships made possible through sharing encounters to do with food. While we recognise the challenges and question the desirability of providing an à la carte experience at mealtimes, responsive care would lead staff to take into account particular likes and dislikes in the preparation of food and to offer alternatives if a child really doesn't like something. 'Knowing how somebody likes their food or drink and paying attention to detail (e.g. what cheese you like and how you like it on your toast) is a way of showing you care' (Punch et al, 2009: 27). Similarly, preparing a special supper, snack or soup when you are ill is experienced as an act of care, 'often less because of the food per se than because of the personal attentiveness and connection involved in these acts of providing' (Punch et al, 2009: 27). Small things like a staff member being able to produce a sweet or a bar of chocolate at an appropriate moment when a child might be tired or upset are easy but powerful ways to give a message to children and young people that they are cared for.

Clothing

Clothing, like food, is another basic human need. In residential child care, however, considerations of clothing have shifted from a needs perspective to a rights perspective. Children and young people have clothing grants allocated to them by placing local authorities and, of course, it is right that they should have access to sufficient funds to ensure that they are well kitted out and have access to clothing that allows them to feel on a par with their peers.

One of the problems with clothing grants, however, is that a rights way of thinking makes it too easy for carers (often under pressure from wider agency policies and assumptions) to hand monies over to children and young people to spend at will, and thereby to relinquish any caring responsibility to be involved in the clothes that children buy and wear. This is not what happens in most families where parents – for a range of financial, practical and stylistic reasons – have some say in their children's decision making about clothing. Similar considerations should be taken into account for children in care. This isn't about denying rights or withholding responsibility but is about taking responsibility and showing care. Again, we have to go back somewhat in the literature to find this point made, but Burmeister makes the case very clearly when she says that when the carer 'conveys to the child that his clothing is important, that is, how it is obtained for him, how kept up and organised, then the youngster feels that *he* is important to the houseparent too' (1960: 65)

Carers ought to be actively involved in children's and young people's clothing needs, checking length and waist size, proffering opinions about what item they think suits best and giving guidance on the financial implications of any purchase. They also need to ensure that any monies that are available are not spent on two pairs of the latest designer footwear, leaving nothing for sports kit or outdoor wear that will allow children and young people to access a range of activities or opportunities.

Systems in place for washing children's clothes can also act to give particular messages. While it is right that children and young people learn at the appropriate point how to use a washing machine and how to iron their clothes, procedures around this should not become dogmatic. As any parent knows, getting children to take responsibility for their own laundry tends to be, at best, a work in progress; there is a necessary and proper fallback position where carers take some responsibility for such matters. There is also something nice about having freshly laundered and ironed clothes ready for a child when they get up to go to school in the morning. As with food, carers can give strong messages of care by intervening to ensure that children have their favourite jeans washed and ready for them for the weekend and that sports gear is washed and folded away ready for the next PE lesson.

Summary

Bringing up children is, and should be, characterised by intimate, loving and nurturing relationships. Dependency is an appropriate facet of all caring relationships – regardless of age and stage of development – and an essential component in caring for children, with the aim that they gradually become more self-sufficient and competent. Policies and practices ought to support the development of appropriate, intimate and safe cultures in residential child care. Experiencing unconditional and consistent care is powerful, therapeutic and life lasting. Residential care, through the intimacy and normality of shared everyday experiences, offers significant opportunities for children and young people to develop a positive sense of self and self-worth. For them to do so requires that carers develop and feel comfortable with what Boddy (2011) calls a 'professional heart', which blends an appropriate sense of purpose with the emotional dimensions that are vital to bringing up children.

Returning to the scenario

The opening case scenario offers an example of responsive care. Ian, the manager, realises that Tony has not showered before getting dressed to go clothes shopping. This shows in his unkempt appearance. Adam, the care worker, has, for whatever reason, not taken sufficient responsibility to ensure that Tony has showered. Showering and generally taking a bit of time to get ready becomes significant for boys of Tony's age – probably approaching puberty – with what this entails in terms of paying attention to personal hygiene, especially if he is to be trying on new clothes. Most 13-year-old boys are also likely to be conscious of their appearance, but may require a bit of prompting from those around them to ensure that they get this right. Carers need to take a proactive role in this.

Seeing his grumpy demeanour, knowing how he responds to adults, and aware of the kind of relationships that each of the actors have with one another, Ian employs a humorous approach to get his message over to both Tony and Adam. Tussling Tony's hair in a naturalistic way allows him to make a physical and caring connection. There may have been a range of circumstances that contributed to Tony not being suitably cared for that morning and, as in any family setting, it can be helpful if a partner (or in the case of residential child care, a colleague) can point out lapses. As with most situations in residential child care, drawing attention to some of Adam's shortfalls in this scenario is best done in a lifespace context. Ian responds in the moment to the situation in front of him and uses humour to address it in a way that ensures that Adam is aware of his concerns but is able to hear these in a non-blaming way.

Tony is also made to feel very much part of the developing episode. His mood becomes more playful and he is able to enter into the spirit of Ian's play-acting. He is able to respond, happily, to Ian's request to sort himself out before he goes shopping. Setting out on the trip in a good mood and feeling good about his appearance is likely to ensure that the shopping trip passes off successfully.

Thoughts for practice

Staff members might be encouraged to think about what it feels like to be cared for and whether care practices in their workplace provide children with suitable opportunities to experience the kind of care that they themselves value.

Staff teams might discuss whether it is OK to talk about loving children you work with. Discussion threads on CYC-Net might provide a good starting point for such a discussion: www.cyc-net.org/threads/iloveyou.html. Consider what policies exist around touching children and other potentially intimate encounters. Are these really policies or merely ingrained assumptions? What are the implications of these on children's care? A discussion thread on touch is also available on CYC-Net: www.cyc-net.org/threads/touch.html

In what ways might your home be described as one that smiles, with props that invite and space that allows? What do institutional practices do or not do to make children and young people feel cared for?

Think about the role that food plays in children feeling cared for, and what rituals surround the preparation and eating of food. How might food be used to help individual children feel special by, for instance, knowing what their favourite meal is and their particular likes and dislikes?

Similarly, think about practices around the purchase and washing of clothes and how these affect a child or young person's sense of feeling cared for.

Further reading

Steckley and Smith begin to discuss ideas of care from a care ethics perspective in:

Steckley, L. and Smith, M. (2011) 'Care ethics in residential child care: a different voice', *Ethics and Social Welfare*, vol 5, no 2, pp 181–95.

Nel Noddings, although primarily a philosopher of education, has some very interesting and mostly accessible things to say about care. See:

Noddings, N. (2002a) *Starting at home: caring and social policy*, Berkeley, CA: University of California Press.

A helpful summary of the Punch et al (2009) research on food practices, which offers wider insights into the nature of care, is available at:

www.ncb.org.uk/media/518085/ncercc_stirling_food_staffhandbook.pdf

4

Healthy: a sense of wellbeing

Scenario

Linsey, a young white woman is coming up 17. She has been in and out of care since she was three. Her mother, Jan, is a chaotic alcoholic who has had regular house moves interspersed with periods of homelessness. Over the years Jan has made intermittent, generally unplanned contact with Linsey. Although their relationship is fractious, there is an obvious bond between them, although they are more like rivalrous adolescents than mother and daughter. Professionals feel that Jan's contact just upsets Linsey and are concerned that Linsey is exposed to drink, drugs and sexual exploitation when in her mother's company.

Linsey was placed in secure accommodation when she was 14 due to the breakdown of every other placement she had been in. She mostly flourished there. She is intelligent, engaging and witty, and established close relationships with a number of staff members. However, attempts to move her out of the secure unit met with variable levels of success and she would go missing, often for extended periods, and when found it was generally in the company of potentially abusive adults and invariably under the influence of drink and drugs. On her return from such episodes her physical condition had visibly deteriorated. She was rarely forthcoming about where she had been or what she had been up to and acted aggressively towards staff members, almost as if to keep them at bay.

Not long after her 16th birthday Linsey goes missing and is arrested, having been involved in assaulting a member of the public. She spends a period on remand in the local women's prison. The secure unit she had been in previously has a step-down facility to help young people move towards more independent living and she is given a place there on her release from prison.

One Friday night she comes downstairs, heavily made up and wearing a particularly short skirt.

Mags, the member of staff on duty, with whom Linsey has a good relationship, tries to engage her in conversation: "So where are you off to, then?"

Linsey (evasively): "Up town. I'm going to meet some friends."

Mags: "Well, you're certainly dressed to kill. Do you not think that skirt is a bit short?"

Linsey: "Naw! What's it to you what I wear, anyway?"

Mags: "Nothing, I suppose. I just don't want you to be drawing too much attention to yourself and getting into bother when you're up town. What time will you be back?"

Linsey: "Eleven o'clock, I suppose … that's what time I always have to be in to this shithole."

Mags: "OK then. I'll see you then. I'm on sleep-over. Take care!"

Eleven o'clock comes and goes with no sign of Linsey. She isn't answering her mobile phone. Around one in the morning, the police phone to say they have found Linsey wandering the main city centre street, drunk and abusing passers-by. They have picked her up and are holding her at the police station until unit staff can pick her up. Mags is woken up and two night staff go off to collect Linsey, returning about half an hour later.

Linsey is in a volatile mood on her return. She is clearly still under the influence of drink and possibly drugs. She looks dishevelled and has obviously fallen over. Her make-up is smudged and she seems to have been crying.

Mags realises she will have to tread carefully: "Dear, dear what a state you're in. What have you been getting up to?"

Linsey doesn't seem to respond directly and is obviously distracted.

Mags goes over to put the kettle on: "Come on, I don't suppose we can go much further until we've both had a cup of tea. Sit yourself down."

Linsey does. Mags asks the night staff to leave them alone and pours a couple of cups of tea.

Once Linsey starts to drink the tea and begins to settle slightly, Mags begins to engage her in conversation: "So, are you going to tell me where you've been?"

Linsey: "I went down to meet this guy. He has a flat near the town. It was minging. He had loads of cheap cider, and some other stuff. It went to my head – I got pure out of it."

Mags: "Did he try and do anything?"

Linsey: "… I don't know …"

Mags: "And, I don't suppose he would have used any contraception if he did …"

Linsey: "I don't know … not that that would matter. I can't have babies anyway."

Mags: "What do you mean by that?"

Linsey: "Well, I've had sex with loads of guys and never use contraception and I've never got pregnant. No wonder, when you think about all the shit I've taken over the years."

Mags: "Has someone told you that?"

Linsey: "No, but there must be some reason …"

Mags: "Well, maybe you've just been lucky, or when you go missing and don't eat properly and get yourself into the kind of states you do, your body's certainly not going to be at its best, but that doesn't mean there's anything seriously wrong. We need to get you checked out … for your own peace of mind as much as anything else. You know, you break my heart getting into situations like this. I just wish you thought as much about yourself as we think about you. Come on, we'll see what we need to do after a night's sleep."

Introduction

Any placement in a residential child care facility represents a formal incursion by the state into the traditionally private domain of family life. One of the main duties that falls upon any parent is to ensure that children's health needs are attended to. In the case of children in residential care, depending on the nature of the legal basis for placement, many of these duties of care are assigned to residential child care workers as agents of the state in its corporate parenting capacity.

In this chapter we consider the physical and mental health issues faced by many children in care and how placement in residential child care might offer an opportunity to address some of these more immediate needs. We locate discussion of children's health needs within their social circumstances and, in particular, within the growing literature on health inequalities (Wilkinson and Pickett, 2009). Increasingly, medical thinking recognises the inadequacy of a primary concern on the prevention of ill health and is shifting focus towards actively promoting a broader sense of wellbeing. Achieving a sense of wellbeing is a social as much as it is a medical process, and we consider how residential care might contribute towards such a goal. This can only really happen within a holistic experience of being and feeling cared for.

The health needs of children in care

Poor health outcomes for children and young people looked after by local authorities are well evidenced and documented, with high levels of long-term illnesses, mental ill health, poor dental health, smoking, poor diet and sleep patterns, alcohol and drug misuse, teenage pregnancy and sexually transmitted infections being reported (Grant et al, 2002). These outcomes can be attributed to a variety of factors. Many children and young people suffer from neglected health while living at home due to frequent changes of address and hence medical practices. Infrequent school attendance may result in missed health checks or immunisations. This does not necessarily improve when they become accommodated, as a result of frequent placement moves and lack of continuity of carers.

A common characteristic among many children and young people at the time they are placed in care is that they are at a point of crisis. Their lifestyles can often be chaotic and include risk-taking behaviour. Health difficulties have often been left unaddressed and have become entrenched. Many minor medical problems, left untreated, can have serious long-term health impacts.

Studies have also shown high rates of mental disorder among looked after and accommodated children and young people. In some respects, this reflects wider social trends where the mental health of children and young people has become a growing cause for concern. Figures from a comprehensive UK study indicate that about 9% of all children and young people experience a mental health disorder (Meltzer, 2000). Among the emotional and psychological problems reported in recent years are increasing rates of eating disorders, an increase in suicide rates among young men, and considerable increases in conditions such as hyperactivity among younger children. Increasing numbers of children diagnosed with an autistic spectrum disorder are also apparent.

This situation is amplified in residential child care. An Office of National Statistics Survey for Scotland (Meltzer et al, 2004) found that 45% of looked after children suffer from a mental health disorder. This confirms more localised studies (Dimigen et al, 1999), which found that many of the children aged 12 and under had mental health disorders at the time of entering care and that many had not received any treatment for these disorders.

The majority of disturbed children placed in care will primarily have either emotional or conduct disorders. Emotional disorders include high levels of anxiety and distress resulting from difficult life experiences. Conduct disorders are often manifest in superficial relationships with others and anti-social behaviour such as violence and lack of consideration for others. Although these two types of presentation can be seen separately, they are often combined (Milligan, 2005).

The social circumstances of children in care

The impoverished conditions of children in care, as well as those of their families, are well documented (Bebbington and Miles, 1989). Berridge and Brodie (1998) identify children in care as among the most disadvantaged in society. In 2003 the Scottish Children's Reporter Administration (SCRA) conducted a small scale study on the case files of those children referred to children's hearings (not necessarily those admitted to residential child care, by which stage difficulties are likely to be even more apparent) in three different geographical areas (SCRA, 2004). The main findings of the study were:

- Almost half of children had physical and/or mental health problems;
- 58% had social, behavioural or emotional difficulties; 33% had experienced physical, sexual or emotional abuse;
- 37% had been neglected or diagnosed with failure to thrive;
- 36% of their parents/carers had mental health problems;
- 43% of children had experience of domestic abuse in their homes; 39% of parents/carers abused alcohol;
- 35% of parents/carers misused drugs.

Children in all three areas studied experienced these problems, despite different levels of affluence and deprivation between geographical locations. Residential child care increasingly works with children and families where social problems such as drug misuse spans generations of a family.

Health inequalities

Public health medicine has identified significant health disparities linked to geography. In certain areas of Glasgow, for instance, male life expectancy at 63 is some 14 years below the UK average. Low life expectancy is linked to social factors such as housing conditions and employment status. The Centre for Social Justice *Breakthrough Glasgow* report (2008) records that the stress of living in deprivation is responsible for premature deaths in deprived communities. Those who live in the poorest areas are nearly three times as likely to be admitted to hospital for depression as those who are not, and are three times more likely to commit suicide. Children from the lowest social strata are more likely to have a mental disorder than those in the top social brackets. The highest rates of mental disorders among children occur among those from families where no parent has ever worked (Hanlon and Carlisle, 2011).

But it is not just poverty that affects children's life chances. Despite often chaotic home circumstances that might entail periodic missing of meals or shortage of basic material goods, few children nowadays experience sustained absolute poverty to the point of malnutrition. An overall improvement in material standards, however, has not had a discernible positive effect on health, and in many respects coincides with an increase in mental health problems.

Wilkinson and Pickett's (2009) work on health inequalities casts some light on why this is the case. They argue that it is not so much poverty as inequality that has an adverse effect on health. Poor societies can be happy and well-adjusted. As the gap between rich and poor increases, however, health and other social problems increase for those on the bottom rungs of the social ladder. A growing body of literature supports the view that widening social inequalities in the UK pose a substantial threat to mental health. For example, data from the UK poverty and social exclusion survey (Payne, 1999) suggest that anyone who experiences poverty and exclusion is at increased risk of suffering from poor mental health. Links between mental and physical health are also increasingly apparent; when stressed or depressed, individuals are more likely to develop heart disease or infections, or to show signs of premature ageing. Stress disrupts the body's balance or homeostasis and attacks its immune system (Wilkinson and Pickett, 2009).

The interplay of social conditions with mental and physical health and the seeming intractability of health problems in poorer communities has led public health doctors such as Hanlon et al (2011) to suggest the need for a very different mindset to be applied to how we understand and respond to health issues. They suggest that the public health problems we now face – such as obesity, enduring health inequalities, the rise in mental distress, and increasingly problematic use of drugs and alcohol – have a common source in the pressures of living in the modern world. The resultant problems can, according to Hanlon and Carlisle (2010), be thought of not as 'diseases' but as 'dis-eases'. People are not at ease with themselves and this state of being is manifest in poor mental and physical health. Hanlon et al suggest that the health and wellbeing issues that confront us can no longer be addressed by conventional forms of thinking, tools or approaches. We face what they call 'an "ingenuity gap" between the medical problems we face and the adequacy of the conceptual tools we can draw upon to address these' (Hanlon et al, 2011). They locate many of these problems in the wider social forces of the modern world.

Living in the modern world

What is thought of as the modern world has roots back to the 17th and 18th century Enlightenment. Modernity was based around a belief in social and scientific progress and a desire for order. The high point of the modern period might be thought to be the post-war years, when there was pretty much full employment and the welfare state had been introduced to tackle social ills. The certainties of an industrial and welfare age, however, have given way to what commentators call variously post-, high-, late-, or liquid modernity. Liquid modernity, according to Bauman (1993), is distinguished from the more 'solid' modernity of the post-war welfare consensus, with its belief in human progress through rational scientific advance, by an increased pace of change and fluidity. Values, too, are fluid; erstwhile points on a moral compass are less clear. Generally, people can be less sure of their place and status in the world.

Specifically, liquid modernity is characterised by consumerism. Consumer society puts value on choice. In reality, though, and despite the rhetoric of capitalism, not everyone can exercise choice as a consumer. People on a low income are the flawed consumers: those who, through little fault of their own, are left behind in a free market economy. They are, nevertheless, subject to the same advertising messages as the rest of us, piling on the pressure to consume. It is this dynamic that might explain the attraction to children in care and their families of the latest mobile phones, the widescreen televisions and the designer gear that can seem to be a feature of poorer individuals and communities. It is one way of attempting to assert some sort of status that they otherwise find it hard to claim. But the pressures of a modern consumerist society are not confined to material goods. Relationships, too, have become commodified. The deep human longing for happiness persistently eludes individuals in poorer communities, as they enter into a series of unfulfilling and transient relationships.

The low social status of poorer individuals and communities is related to a range of physical diseases. A growing literature demonstrates that societies where there has been a growth in free market trends such as consumerism, individualism, competition and inequality can create psychological forms of dislocation to which addictive behaviour is a common adaptive response (Hanlon, Carlisle and Henderson, 2011). Drug use is more common in more unequal societies (Wilkinson and Pickett, 2009). As we have already noted, children in care often come from families where addiction of some sort is a problem. It is to addictions and their impact on children in care that we now turn.

Addictions

Substance misuse can lead to two categories of harm. The first of these stems from the health problems caused by its direct biological effects. Examples of these would be the sharing of needles among those who inject heroin and the increased risk of blood-borne viruses as a result, and drinking alcohol to excess over many years leading to cirrhosis and foetal alcohol syndrome. This has tangible effects for many children in care who have lost family members and have to cope with those losses. 'The second category of harm is not the direct result of the biological effects of drugs, but has to do with the wider effects of addictive behaviour on individuals, their families and society in general' (Hanlon et al, 2011). The key concept here – and perhaps the indicator of addiction – is one of involvement in substance use leading to harm, reflecting the reality that many of us use drugs of one sort or another in our daily lives, but manage to do so with few ill-effects on ourselves or others. For many children in care, their parents' addiction to drink or drugs can have major adverse effects on their emotional and physical wellbeing.

Effects of addictions on children and families

Attachment theory is constructed around the emotional availability of parents for their children. Consistent availability and picking up and responding to the cues prompted by mutual interaction encourage a parent's atunement to a child's internal mental states, a dynamic that Howe (2005) describes as 'mind-mindedness'. This capacity to pick up and respond to mental cues forms the basis of a child's developing psychological adjustment.

Addiction to drink or drugs can become an addicted parent's primary concern; the need for a fix becomes more powerful than the instinct to respond to their child's needs. At one level this can be manifest in neglect of material needs and routines. At another level the mind-altering effects of substance abuse get in the way of and distort the capacity for accurate attunement to a child's emotional needs. The child, as a consequence, cannot rely on predictable, dependable or appropriate responses. The result is distorted, disrupted and disturbed parent–child relationships (Howe, 2005). Depression similarly distorts the parent–child relationship, often being manifest in withdrawal, under-stimulation and disengagement. The increasing numbers of children entering residential child care from families with addiction problems, thus, do so lacking many of the building blocks for successful emotional adjustment and wellbeing.

Low socioeconomic status and high social stress are also linked with more overt abuse. Conditions such as depression and alcoholism are associated with an increased incidence of physical abuse. Physically abused children can present a range of physical and emotional symptoms of that abuse (Howe, 2005). Sexual abuse, too, is highly correlated with family stress and disorganisation and a lack of appropriate household boundaries, which can be manifest in the coming and going of a series of undesirable individuals. Again, sexual abuse can be implicated in a range of subsequent emotional difficulties, although it should not be assumed that this is inevitable. How children (and adults) respond to sexual abuse will depend on a range of factors such as previous and subsequent experience, personal resilience and how others react to them. The label or even the suspicion of sexual abuse can, sometimes, result in carers thinking that this is something that requires a very specialist understanding and treatment, which in turn can get in the way of them responding through the medium of everyday care and nurture.

The general consequence of children being brought up in families where their basic safety needs have not been met, or their attachments disrupted or distorted, is a lack of an appropriate sense of self-worth. This can be reflected in different types of what Anglin (2002) terms pain-based behaviour, manifest in withdrawal, acting out or, on occasion, self-harm. It can also be manifest in reckless behaviour and a quest for immediate gratification. Wilkinson and Pickett (2009) identify reckless behaviour as happening when individuals experience a lack of hope for the future. Thus, children in care and other family members get involved in offending, drug and alcohol consumption and inappropriate sexual relationships, not so much because they don't know that such behaviours are wrong or bad for them, but because they see little reason not to.

The ingenuity gap

As previously noted, Hanlon et al (2011) identify an ingenuity gap in how we think about and address health issues generally. There is perhaps a similar gap that needs to be considered in the context of residential child care, suggesting a need to think differently about what it is to be healthy and how we might best help children in care to be so. There is no doubt that many of the initiatives set up over the past decade to address the health needs of children in care have been successful at a basic level. A more coordinated approach, often with specialist looked after children's nurses at its centre, has ensured that the kind of gaps in basic health provision that used to exist for children in care are far more rare. The establishment of child and adolescent mental health services has also built up a level of expertise and support for staff working with children and young people's emotional difficulties. Aspects of the drive to encourage health-promoting units, such as the emphasis on areas of diet and physical activity, are also welcome.

The growing understanding of the extent of the links between mental and physical health, however, suggests the need for a broader appreciation of what constitutes good health and how it might be encouraged more than has often been the case in conventional medicine or health promotion. Most people, including children, know that they ought to eat five portions of fruit or vegetables a day. They know the risks of inappropriate sexual contact. Health education, however, is only a small part of the answer in respect of changing lifestyles. Health promotion initiatives on their own are unlikely to have much impact unless children begin to feel that they lend some meaning to their own circumstances. A healthy residential home might in fact be one that, in the context of good enough dietary planning, provides children with plentiful supplies of chocolate spread and popcorn and keeps chips on the menu a couple of times a week, if to do so is going to help children enjoy mealtimes. It might even turn a blind eye to a child or young person having a cigarette, if smoking has become for them a habitual recourse at times of stress. In fact, to do so might avert less adaptive responses to stress such as acting out or running off.

Wellbeing

There is a growing focus across academic disciplines, from psychology (Seligman, 2002; Nettle, 2005) and philosophy (for example, Vanier, 2001) to economics (Layard, 2006), on a concept or concepts of wellbeing or happiness. The ideas of happiness or flourishing and attainment of what might be thought of as 'a good life' can be traced back to the Greek philosopher, Aristotle. Vanier (2001) considers that human beings are made for happiness. The demands and conditions of the modern world, however – as identified above – can get in the way of this.

Wellbeing is a diffuse and contested concept although:

> most researchers agree about its domains; physical wellbeing;
> material wellbeing; social wellbeing; development and activity;
> emotional wellbeing. The elements can be paraphrased as physical
> health, income and wealth, relationships, meaningful work and
> leisure, personal stability and (lack of) depression. Mental health is
> increasingly seen as fundamental to overall health and wellbeing.
> (Eichsteller and Holthoff, 2010: 87)

Nettle (2005) suggests that expectations of happiness in our society may be unrealistically high, and consumer culture certainly encourages us to believe in a happy, shiny existence that few really attain. We risk building in disappointment when we don't achieve what we are encouraged to believe is possible in television ads. Children in care are perhaps particularly vulnerable to unrealistic messages of what they think they should expect from life. Happiness isn't a 'once and for all' feeling but a life's journey, which includes ups and downs, but within which the overall outlook is generally positive and the overall trajectory generally upwards. This does not come about merely through positive thinking – aspects of genetic predisposition, as well as early life experience can also influence an individual's state of mind. But it may offer pointers as to how we approach our work with children and young people, suggesting a general strengths-based rather than a deficit-based approach.

Salutogenesis

The health sociologist Antonovsky (1996) offers salutogenesis as an alternative to more conventional medical concepts, which are concerned with disease. Salutogenesis focuses on the factors that support human health and wellbeing (Eichsteller and Holthoff, 2010). A central idea in Antonovsky's work is what he identifies as an individual's achievement (or non-achievement) of a sense of coherence, which he identifies as being fundamentally implicated in health. Whether or not stress will be manifest in ill health is determined by the extent to which it violates an individual's sense of coherence. Coherence itself has three components:

- comprehensibility: a belief that things happen in an orderly and predictable fashion and a sense that you can understand events in your life and reasonably predict what will happen in the future;
- manageability: a belief that you have the skills or ability, the support, the help, or the resources necessary to take care of things, and that things are manageable and within your control;
- meaningfulness: a belief that things in life are interesting and a source of satisfaction, that things are really worth it and that there is good reason or purpose to care about what happens.

According to Antonovsky, the third element, meaningfulness, is the most important. If a person believes there is no reason to persist or survive and confront challenges – if they have no sense of meaning – then they will have no motivation to comprehend and manage events. The converse of this, as Antonovsky demonstrates in his research, is that a sense of coherence predicts positive health outcomes.

Positive psychology

Psychology as a discipline has historically focused on mental distress. More recent developments within what is termed positive psychology seek to realign the discipline's focus away from pathology, victimology and mental illness towards an emphasis on mental health and what might sustain this. Seligman (2002), one of the foremost proponents of positive psychology, suggests that happiness and its spin-offs in terms of mental health can be cultivated at emotional, behavioural and institutional levels. Positive psychology would fit with a strengths-based orientation and might help shift residential child care away from what can appear to be its pre-eminent concern with children's difficulties. This is not to suggest that many of these difficulties are unreal *or not* well entrenched, nor that they are *likely* to be amenable to 'just be happy' exhortations. Positive psychology can, understandably, be accused of underestimating the economic and other structural impediments that individuals and communities face (Ferguson, 2008). In emphasising the importance of fulfilling activity and relationships within a context of everyday living, however, it may have something to offer in terms of setting a direction for residential child care.

More positive psychological orientations might suggest a caveat to dominant ideas of how children can be helped to overcome adversity, which is generally through a focus on their problems and a notion of 'expert' treatments to deal with these. Furedi (2003) argues that in the modern world health has become a consumer commodity, peddled by a growing army of therapists. Social work buys into this to a large extent through what can be, at times, a simplistic adoption of psychologically based assumptions that the behaviours of children in care are grounded in past trauma. We have already acknowledged that the social circumstances of children in care can and do, indeed, lead to emotional and physical symptoms. Some children, however, also manage to display quite remarkable resilience in the face of such adversity, and to focus primarily on their difficulties can be disabling for them and can impede staff from responding creatively to their wider developmental needs.

Even in cases where past experience undoubtedly has had a detrimental impact on children's current functioning, questions arise around how best to respond to these difficulties. In this respect the term 'therapeutic' is, arguably, overused in residential care. Poorly understood therapeutic approaches can, according to Furedi (2003) lead people to become stuck in their problems rather than to seek to overcome them. From his perspective, distress in modern society has become something not to be lived with or lived through, but a condition that requires treatment. Very often, our view of treatment in residential care borrows, at often very simplistic levels, from such psychological or therapeutic discourses. And, in fact, evidence of the effectiveness of treatment models in residential child care is modest (Gharabaghi, 2011). So, while some psychological insights might be helpful, the most effective therapy that residential child care can provide is in the provision of quality everyday care, predicated upon a strong sense of purpose, along with authoritative and committed personal relationships.

Strengths and solution-focused approaches can be helpful in everyday engagement with young people in care. Their focus on the here and now and the preferred future of the young person allows a different type of conversation to happen between young people and carers, in that there is less focus on the problems of the past and on attempts to understand why things happened. For example, to engage children in discussion around why their parents appear to choose alcohol and drugs before them may never be fully answered or understood. It may be better replaced with something along the lines of: 'So all these difficult and hurtful things have happened to you and we may never fully understand why. In what ways would you like things to be different now? What is, or could be, happening for you, to help you begin to think about a different sort of future?'

Relationships

A sense of wellbeing is fundamentally linked to the quality of relationships an individual can draw upon. Lane (2001), a political scientist, has suggested that our static or diminished sense of happiness in the modern world is a consequence of a decline of companionship. Layard (2006) further speculates about the increasing misery caused by inharmonious social relations, uncertainties associated with living in modern society, and inappropriate life goals. By contrast, having friends, being married, belonging to a religious group or other association and being able to call upon social support at times of need are all factors that are protective of health (Wilkinson and Pickett, 2009). Human life unfolds within a relational context that is fundamental to a sense of meaning. Committed relationships are essential in giving our lives the kind of meaning from which a sense of wellbeing can emerge. Again, this challenges residential child care to consider how it supports the kind of committed relationships through which children feel valued and through which they can begin to gain a sense of wellbeing. White (2008) identifies one of the pillars of child care to be significance, which he links to the unconditional commitment of at least one adult throughout a child's upbringing. There are obvious lessons in this, both for placement policies that build in instability and for child protection discourses that view such unconditional and special relationships with suspicion.

Another message from the literature on wellbeing is around a general sense of satisfaction with life and what it has to offer. This might suggest the setting of goals that are possible, because individual wellbeing is viewed less as a reachable goal and more as a state that can emerge when an individual is making good progress towards his or her life goals. Again, this would link the attainment of a sense of wellbeing to the wider programme of a residential home, where children ought to be encouraged to find a sense of purpose and to feel hopeful that they can make realistic progress towards their goals.

Spirituality

Our growing understanding of the importance of individuals experiencing a sense of wellbeing revolves around elements of meaning, purpose and affirming relationships. For many people, a sense of meaning is gained through having a spiritual dimension in their lives. The modern world often eschews spirituality, linking it – rightly or wrongly – to organised religion. Social work as a profession, despite having long roots in religious tradition, has adopted largely secular ways of viewing the world.

There is, however, a growing awareness of the important role that a spiritual dimension can play in giving meaning to people's lives and in contributing to a sense of wellbeing. Spirituality relates to the way in which people understand and live their lives in view of their sense of ultimate meaning and value. 'It can be seen as comprising elements of *meaning, purpose, value, hope, love* and for some people, *a connection to a higher power* or something greater than self' (Swinton, 2005 [italics in original]). Swinton suggests that children are naturally spiritual – that they have an inherent sense of awe, wonder and acceptance of things beyond their understanding.

The importance of a spiritual dimension in enhancing a person's wellbeing is lent weight by a growing evidence base that indicates a positive correlation between spirituality and mental health. Religion and spirituality have been shown to be beneficial on a number of levels and in relation to a wide variety of health conditions, including protection against depression and anxiety. Specifically, spirituality seems to help reframe mental health problems in positive ways, by offering qualities of hope, value, meaning and purpose to people's lives (Swinton, 2005).

As indicated above, a possible spiritual dimension of children's lives in residential care has not been readily accommodated in recent decades, being reduced, at best, to expectations to maintain any pre-existing family religious observance. Carers perhaps need to be more open to and proactive in facilitating some element of spiritual connection for children and young people.

A lifespace approach

As with just about every other aspect of this book we are drawn back to a lifespace approach to articulate what all of this foregoing discussion might mean for residential child care. A lifespace approach to health issues was articulated as far back as the turn of the 20th century by Jane Addams, one of the pioneering figures in American social work. In her work in the Hull House settlement in Chicago, Addams made the point that:

> ... to put information into readable form is not nearly enough. It is to confuse a simple statement of knowledge with its application. Permit me to illustrate from a group of Italian women who bring their under-developed children several times a week to Hull House for sanitary treatment, under the direction of a physician. It has been possible to teach some of these women to feed their children oatmeal instead of tea-soaked bread, but it has been done, not by statement at all but by a series of gay little Sunday morning breakfasts given to a group of them in the Hull House nursery. A nutritious diet was then substituted for an inferior one by a social method. (Jane Addams in 1899: cited by Magnuson, 2003: xxi)

There are lessons in this for contemporary residential child care. It is not enough to ensure that children are told what is good (or bad) for them – they have to experience and recognise the benefits of changing their behaviours in the context of their everyday living and alongside those who care for them. This places an onus on staff to model not just what might be thought of as healthy lifestyles but also healthy relationships and expectations. Healthy living follows on from children feeling safe, nurtured and achieving through receipt of quality holistic care.

Supporting healthy staff

If one of the aims of residential child care is to help children achieve a sense of wellbeing, and if we accept that there are strong social and relational dimensions to this, then it makes sense that we are also concerned about the wellbeing of the staff who care for children. Those of us who have worked for many years in residential child care can identify aspects of the residential lifestyle that are less than healthy. The cumulative stress of working with children's anxieties and acting out could be manifest in cultures of heavy smoking and drinking, and often in premature death in service. In present day managerial cultures, staff members feel uncertain about the control they have over their work and prey to often critical and blaming external cultures. They often do not feel understood or valued. Such cultures are not conducive to carers' good mental or physical health, which, in turn, makes it more difficult to promote or model healthy living messages. So, a proper concern for children's wellbeing ought to extend to ensuring that they are cared for by individuals who themselves feel valued and emotionally 'contained' by their employing agency.

Summary

In recent years, greater attention has been paid to the health needs of children in care. This is evident in the growth in services such as looked after children's nurses and child and adolescent mental health services. Ensuring that the basic medical, dental and mental health needs of children and young people are met ought to be a central concern for residential care workers. However, current thinking on health and wellbeing moves beyond interventions with particular children and young people to locate concerns about their wellbeing within wider social circumstances. Inequality is a major determinant of a range of social and medical ills. Children and adults who lack a sense of meaning, coherence and hope for the future are more likely to engage in reckless behaviours and to turn to drink and drugs to dull the sense of dis-ease in their lives. Lifestyle issues are, in turn, likely to manifest in poorer physical and mental health. Carers therefore need to think holistically about health needs. More than anything, they need to try and instil in young people a sense of worth and of being valued, as it is only then that they will be in a position to make appropriate choices about their health needs.

Returning to the scenario

This case highlights the interplay between social conditions and mental and physical health. For whatever reason, Jan has not been able to develop a suitably mindful understanding of Linsey's needs as different from her own. This has led to distorted patterns of attachment, where Linsey cannot rely on her mother to protect her or to contain her feelings of anxiety.

Linsey has shown that she can be settled and happy when in secure accommodation. Outside this setting, however, she is prey to a range of demands and pressures from the outside world, compounded by her transitional stage, in which she must be wondering what the future holds. Bombarded by images of carefree, idealised lifestyles and relationships promised by the media in a consumer society, she is aware that she will struggle to achieve these. In her more positive periods she sometimes thinks that she might get a job and maybe a flat of her own and settle down, but at other times the future is just too bleak and scary. She seeks excitement but also escape in running off, and through drink and drugs. This lifestyle leads her into inappropriate and probably largely unsatisfying sexual relationships. Like many teenage girls who have not experienced consistent love themselves, she has obviously given thought to having a baby, perhaps to fulfil this need for love. The thought that she may not be able to troubles her, but may also lead her into even less discriminate sexual behaviour.

Linsey has little to look forward to; little sense of meaning or coherence in her life. An instrumental approach to caring for her might consider ensuring that she receives drugs and alcohol counselling, or sex education and contraceptive advice. She may or may not derive some benefit from such interventions. But for the care staff dealing with her at the point of her distress, there is perhaps little that they can do other than to 'hang in' with her and to reinforce messages that she is liked and that she has worth, in the hope that someday she might begin to believe this.

Thoughts for practice

At a practical level, make sure that a child or young person is signed up with a GP practice; if possible, one where they have received health care in the past. Give specific attention to following up on any health issues identified during medical check-ups, as small medical problems can, if left untreated, lead to problems in later life. Link in with local looked after children's health initiatives, especially the looked after children's nurse.

Ensuring good dental health can have a knock-on effect on a young person's self-esteem. Work out when they were last seen for a dental check-up, arrange for them to be signed on with a local dentist, make an appointment and then go with them to help alleviate fears about going to the dentist. Braces to straighten teeth are increasingly regarded as a bit of a fashion symbol.

Think about menus and whether these give appropriate messages about healthy but also enjoyable eating. Identify what special meals a child or young person likes and how these might be included within an overall approach to healthy eating.

Exercise can help young people feel better about themselves. Work out a daily and weekly exercise regime with each child or young person and for resident groups and, if possible, join in with them to help reinforce positive relationship building and a healthy lifestyle.

Talking to young people about sex is not like talking to them about the weather. It can be uncomfortable and this can lead some staff members to avoid it. Tactfully, seek appropriate opportunities for discussions with the children or young people living in your residential child care centre, school or group home about sexual health and responsibility, perhaps using TV programmes or news stories as prompts.

Similarly, try to use lifespace opportunities to reinforce healthy messages around smoking, drugs and alcohol use, perhaps getting young people to review their life experiences with drugs and alcohol.

Consider how children's (and their families') social circumstances might affect how they feel about themselves and how this may in turn show through in their behaviour. Discuss in care planning meetings and in staff meetings how realistic care planning goals might be and how these might contribute to a child's sense of wellbeing.

Discuss in staff meetings what messages staff lifestyles might model for children in their care.

Further reading

A powerful account of the impact of health inequalities is:

Wilkinson, R. and Pickett, K. (2009) *The spirit level: why more equal societies almost always do better*, London: Allen Lane.

Similar material can be found on: www.equalitytrust.org.uk

Another good web resource from public health doctors is:

www.afternow.co.uk

The sections of David Howe's work on the impact of social circumstances on attachment are useful:

Howe, D. (2005) *Child abuse and neglect: attachment, development and intervention*, Basingstoke: Palgrave Macmillan.

5

Achieving and enjoying: education in its widest sense

Scenario

A group of children and staff – a combination of teachers and care staff – from a residential school are on a cycling holiday over the summer holiday period. They arrive at one of their planned stops, a youth hostel in a small coastal village. It is a lovely evening. Many of the local youths and visitors are fishing from the pier. Knowing from previous trips that this was a likely activity, the staff have packed some hand lines. Once they have settled into the hostel the group decides to go fishing.

"OK," says Mr Turnbull, one of the teachers (who is known and referred to by all of the children as Tumsh), "a fiver [five pounds] to anyone who can catch a kipper." Brendan is a streetwise 14-year-old. He has been brought up in a local authority housing estate on the edge of a large city with ready access to the local countryside. His family is from a travelling background. His father has served a number of prison sentences and his mother settled in their current home area a number of years ago. Brendan lives a sort of Huckleberry Finn lifestyle there, camping out; often just staying out. He has a good knowledge of and interest in birds and animals and nature generally. He has spent much of the holiday pointing out birds and wildlife to the group. He sidles up to Mr Turnbull.

Brendan: "You can't catch a kipper, Tumsh."

Mr Turnbull: "Of course you can, Brendan, how else do you think you get them? What does anyone else think? You can catch a kipper can't you?"

The other children in the group seem a bit unsure.

Brendan (insistent): "No, you can't catch kippers – they're smoked herring."

Mr Turnbull: "OK, we'll see – a fiver for anyone who can catch a kipper."

As the children make their way down to the pier, two of the staff head to the shops in the local village to see if they can buy a kipper. They can't, but do come across a candy kipper, which they buy. They return to the pier where Brendan and some of the other boys have dropped their hand lines off the pier.

Mr Turnbull approaches one of the other boys and lets him know what is going on. He instructs this other lad to climb down under the pier and to attach the candy kipper to Brendan's line.

One of the other members of staff creates the necessary distraction by calling for a group photograph. Once the photo has been taken the boys return to their lines. Brendan pulls his up to find the candy kipper hanging, somewhat precariously, on his hook.

Brendan: "Tumsh you … OK that's a fiver you owe me …"

The whole group falls around laughing.

Introduction

Achieving is about accomplishing something. In that sense it helps develop the skills to do well in life. Niss claims that achievement helps us 'develop a positive self-esteem, feelings of acceptance, adequacy and self-worth' (1999). While for children achievement is, typically, associated with learning in school, it occurs and ought to be promoted in all aspects of their lives. Children and young people can achieve through involvement in activities, daily life events, sports, cultural activities and community participation. Achievement experiences are likely to be enhanced if they are also enjoyable. Noddings argues that 'Happiness and education are, properly, intimately connected. Happiness should be an aim of education, and a good education should contribute significantly to personal and collective happiness' (2003: 1). In this chapter, we consider what education is, and also what happiness is, and then how the two might come together.

The nature of education

Philosophers have debated the nature and purpose of education over centuries. Rousseau, in the 18th century, argued that education should follow a natural model, taking its cue from pupils' readiness to learn. The role of the educator in such circumstances was to respond to and facilitate opportunities for learning as they emerged in the growing child. Robert Owen, in his New Lanark model community, took a broader view and saw education as being at the heart of social change. His educational philosophy drew on the teachings of European pedagogues, such as the Swiss Johann

Pestalozzi. A. S. Neill, the Scottish educationalist who established Summerhill School in Suffolk in the 1920s, believed that a child's happiness should be the overarching consideration in decisions about their upbringing, and that this happiness grew from a sense of personal freedom (Neill, 1966)

Progressive educational approaches, however, have for the most part been fairly rare. Most educational provision, especially for poorer children, was of a basic 'chalk and talk' variety. The purpose of care institutions, historically, was to feed, train in work habits and give a basic education to children. They were to be prepared for particular stations in life: boys for manual labour or the armed forces and girls for domestic service. A focus on moral rectitude could be manifest in harsh discipline.

Such limiting ideas of education have re-emerged in late capitalist societies where education is generally restricted to a narrow view of schooling. Dominant forms of education reflect what the Brazilian educator, Paulo Freire (1972), calls a 'banking model', whereby education is thought of as the acquisition of facts transmitted from 'expert' teachers to passive learners. Knowledge is stored or 'banked' in learners' heads until it needs to be regurgitated for the purposes of examinations. While few educationalists would go along with such a view of education, it is what is encouraged in systems that are fundamentally based around formal qualifications.

The trend towards equating education with formal qualifications has developed apace in recent decades, where there have been moves to standardise curricula and to limit less traditional approaches to education. A predominant emphasis has been placed on basic academic subjects, premised on claims that this is what employers want. This is not to minimise the importance of a solid grounding in subjects such as English and arithmetic – these form the basis for most subsequent learning. The issue is that they need to be made accessible to children and young people in ways that capture their imagination and make sense to them.

Much of the political emphasis on education is formulated in terms of how it might contribute to accreditation within narrow curricular boundaries and an assumption that this can be linked to subsequent economic productivity and growth. This is a notion of what Lister (2003) calls the 'social investment state'. Such a conception of education can be critiqued on account of its conception of the child as a future worker-citizen rather than as a democratic-citizen of the present. At another more practical level, views of education that focus on the attainment of qualifications make assumptions about the goals of education by focusing on its extrinsic worth as a passport into the job market and economic productivity. This represents a questionable assumption at the best of times, and one that becomes decreasingly sustainable at times of economic recession when jobs are less accessible.

Education of children in care

For a variety of reasons many children in care struggle with an educational system so focused on examinations and qualifications. They may have moved from school to school, following house moves, and failed to settle in any one for long enough to experience the level of continuity required to master basic concepts. They may have fallen out with teachers or peers and been excluded from school, or they may have specific learning challenges that make it more difficult for them to take in learning as readily as some of their peers. Past experiences at school may have resulted in them becoming oppositional, unmotivated or underachieving when confronted by those trying to engage them in any kind of learning process. These children or young people become defined by the system as reluctant – reluctant to engage, reluctant to go along, perhaps reluctant to 'give it a try'. While 'reluctant' may be used to explain oppositional, unmotivated or challenging behaviour, it is perhaps more helpful to think of such young people as 'hesitant to engage' with whatever it is they are being asked to do. Oppositional behaviour may be the result of fear through association with previous experiences, perhaps because the young person does not feel (or is not) very capable. Thus, in such situations young people may have learned that if they behave as troublesome, incapable or disengaged, they will be able to exit such situations more quickly. The upshot of these combinations of circumstances is that the educational outcomes for children in care are significantly poorer than for the general population of children.

Over the past decade or so, children in care have been given a far more prominent political profile than previously. In particular, their record of educational underachievement has been recognised and some steps taken to improve this. Jackson and Simon (2006) note that progressing educationally is associated with improvements in mental and physical health, employment, income, housing, family life, absence of addiction problems and a lower risk of involvement with the criminal justice system. A concern to address the educational inequalities apparent between looked after children and children in the wider community has, rightly, permeated recent policy and guidance in this area (Francis, 2006).

Foremost among such policies was the Quality Protects initiative, which ran in England and Wales from 1998 until 2004 and set particular objectives for local authorities with respect to the education of children in care. In Scotland, Learning with Care materials (Connelly et al, 2003) were developed with the aim of helping carers improve the educational attainment of children in care. At a tertiary level, the Buttle Trust charity has established initiatives to support children in care to enter and hold down university places. Initiatives of this sort certainly give a focus to educational improvements for children in care and bring with them resources for practical efforts to support and enrich children's educational experiences and improve qualification rates.

Political initiatives have not been particularly successful, however. Jackson (2006) argues that Quality Protects failed to address structural constraints on residential care and that its objectives did not match what a good parent might expect for their child. *Care matters* (DES, 2006) and *We can and must do better* (Scottish Government, 2007) acknowledge that the gap in achievement between children in care and the wider population is not reducing but, if anything, may be widening.

A downside to government interest in and scrutiny of education is that, at a time when there is perhaps a need to think more creatively about education, schools and school systems have become caught up in a culture of externally imposed demands and regulation. The result of this has been 'League Tables, failing schools, schools put in to special measures, Literacy Hour, Numeracy Hour, paperwork and yet more paperwork for teachers, followed by overbearing and damaging inspections' (Lane, 2008).

The failure of initiatives to improve the education of children in care may not be as successful as hoped for largely because, like so many government initiatives, they look for technical and instrumental answers to complex social problems. While some looked after children do achieve educationally and should have appropriately high expectations placed upon them by social workers and carers – something that has not always been the case (Jackson, 1987) – aspirations towards a greater parity in the outcomes for children in and out of the care system are not amenable to simple political fixes. The educational difficulties of children in care are deep seated. Clough et al (2006) note how the best efforts of staff in residential care can be compromised by the social circumstances of children's families, or indeed by a lack of support from local education authorities. Berridge makes a similar point, arguing that while:

> some looked-after pupils no doubt could and should do better at school … [their] educational problems are more complex and deeply entrenched than is usually assumed, and the explanations more structural in origin. … It is disingenuous therefore to attribute the poor academic results of looked-after children mainly to inadequacies in social work (and not schools, interestingly), which has often occurred. (2006: 3–4)

Forrester (2008) argues that attempts to draw comparisons between children in care and the wider population of children are misguided, and that children's outcomes across a range of measures do in fact improve during time spent in care. This should not suggest that care is doing as good a job as it might, but it does expose some of the simplistic assumptions on which much recent policy has been based.

Another problem with political initiatives designed to improve the education of children in care is that while many of these children will possess a natural intelligence and creativity in different spheres, they never manage entirely to get to grips with what might be thought of as 'the basics'. Conventional school curricula often have little relevance or meaning to children from poorer backgrounds (Glasser, 1969). Noddings (1992) argues that a view of education based around traditional verbal and mathematical curricula is not suited to those children whose talents may lie in different areas. A very traditional, classroom-based view of education has marginalised other learning opportunities in residential care. Many residential schools, for instance, used to have trade departments where children (generally boys) could learn the rudiments of joinery, painting and decorating, gardening or car mechanics from tradesmen employed to teach these skills. Acquiring competence in these skills, and doing so alongside someone often from a similar social background in an apprenticeship-type model, was a very worthwhile experience for many young people.

There are signs of a changing political focus. In Scotland, for instance, training materials based around a broad developmental view of children's educational needs and stressing the need for educationally rich care environments have followed on from the report *We can and must do better* (Scottish Government, 2007). There are also signs across the UK of a loosening of the tight curricular controls that have been placed upon education. In Scotland, *Curriculum for excellence* (Scottish Executive, 2004), which is now being implemented, states its central purpose as enabling all children to become successful learners, confident individuals, effective contributors and responsible citizens; thus embracing 'a broad view of education, which focuses on the development of the whole person in a social setting' (Bloomer, 2008: 32). In many respects, good residential schools always operated to such a model, whereby trade departments, for instance, might provide a means through which boys could learn basic arithmetical or measurement skills in a non-classroom setting. Outdoor education also provided a forum for learners like Bernard, in the scenario that frames this chapter, to excel in his knowledge of nature in a way that conventional classroom teaching might be less likely to facilitate.

We argue in this book that without dismissing the importance of the classroom experience or of formal qualifications, conceptions of education need to be broadened. Noddings describes education as 'a constellation of encounters, both planned and unplanned, that promote growth through the acquisition of knowledge, skills, understanding and appreciation' (2002a: 283). This is not just geared towards the short-term acquisition of qualifications but to lifelong learning. In a rapidly changing world, a sense of curiosity and a capacity for self-directed learning become important in helping individuals maintain a culture of learning (Boud and Fachikoff, 2007). Education should not merely be a preparation for the future, though. It has intrinsic merits, one of which is linked to a sense of happiness.

The nature of happiness

Like education, the idea of happiness is another notion that one often assumes we understand. We are encouraged in a materialistic world to believe that happiness comes through consumption: through designer clothing, the latest games console, the most up-to-date mobile phone. At another level, we are led to imagine a fluffy sort of happiness held out by advertisers' images of happy, smiley families that many children in care have often not experienced, but to which they nevertheless aspire. Such pictures of happiness are rarely what Seligman (2002) would term 'authentic'. Rather, they equate with a sort of preference satisfaction, whereby people attempt to satisfy material wants, believing that this will contribute to emotional or even spiritual wellbeing. It seldom does.

A more authentic sense of happiness is less easily obtained. It is, nevertheless, something to which we all aspire. As noted in the previous chapter, Vanier suggests that human beings are 'made for happiness'. Aristotle's vision of happiness cannot be measured in primarily material terms, or indeed in measurable terms at all. It is more a sense of human fulfilment or flourishing that derives from being drawn towards an idea of what is good and right. To flourish, we need to develop particular dispositions: what Aristotle called 'virtues'. We become happy through the patient acquisition and practice of virtuous habits. The role of education is to cultivate insights and understandings that allow children to develop into people who can flourish and contribute to society. It involves a wider conception of education than mere classroom learning, to incorporate the cultivation of character.

The end point of our quest for happiness is not just a feeling of personal wellbeing but a sense that we have contributed to a broader social good as members of a society. We reach this state through activity, and specifically through the exercise of thought and reason. While Aristotle recognised that wealth, health and friendship were important, he argued that the exercise of reason was 'the major component of happiness' (Noddings 2003: 10). But happiness doesn't come easily; it 'involves study and discipline' (Vanier, 2001: 21).

In an article on the history of residential care, Webb (2010) offers some challenging arguments about the role of education in such settings. He describes the present system as being beset by what he calls 'insidious leniencies' and lacking wider moral purpose. Drawing on the work of the Italian Marxist, Antonio Gramsci, Webb argues that children need to be provided with clear instruction and direction so that they might be freed from what Gramsci called 'the casual, fortuitous influence of the environment' (Gramsci, quoted in Entwistle, 1979: 57). A rigorous approach to education is thus argued to provide children with a means through which they might overcome structural disadvantages in their lives. Webb's suggestion is that residential child care practice has failed to expect or demand enough of children. It has thus replicated the kind of indulgent parenting styles that are implicated in poor behaviour and low levels of achievement. Webb's arguments raise questions around what might be identified as an overly therapeutic focus in thinking about how we best help children who have been disadvantaged. Rather than constructing arguments that children may not be emotionally ready for education, as has been the case within some social work thinking over the years, education itself is seen as the means through which they can be helped to move on in life. Gharabaghi (2011) makes the case that residential child care ought to move from a primary treatment orientation towards a culture of education.

In reality, at policy and practice levels the lives of many young people in care have, in the past and the present, been limited by a poverty of aspiration or expectation about the kind of experiences to which they ought to have access. Too often, perhaps in the name of normalisation or some misguided notion about not wanting to offer experiences too far removed from children's own backgrounds, residential care can simply reinforce the limitations of their pasts. On the contrary, it should raise the sights of young people and offer new experiences. Another view holds that education is a means by which people, through a process of what Freire calls 'conscientization', come to understand their lives – including the constraints that hold them back – and use this understanding to challenge and change their place in the world. Education thus becomes a liberating force (Freire, 1972).

For education to be worthwhile, it must allow children to enjoy better childhoods than they would without it. Aspects of purposeful education do involve hard work and deferring gratification for the benefit of longer-term rewards. But children's happiness in the present must also count. Their enjoyment of school, and more generally of learning, needs to be considered as both an intrinsic good and a crucial pathway towards better outcomes, including personal and social life outcomes (Thin, 2009).

Bringing education and happiness together

Children are naturally curious about themselves, others and the world around them. We have known for a long time that children learn through play, and that enjoyment and achievement come together. Initial curiosity for some children may have been stifled by health challenges or by life circumstances that have either provided insufficient stimulation or have actively curtailed their curiosity. Conversely, those children who learn well do so best when they enjoy what they are being taught. We work best when we enjoy the work or the challenge and find that what we are doing is not drudgery. According to Glasser (1998) a sense of fun is a human need that is fundamentally implicated in how we learn and achieve in all areas of our lives. Noddings (2003) reinforces this link between learning and fun or happiness, noting that:

> The best homes and schools are happy places. The adults in these happy places recognise that one aim of education (and of life itself) is happiness. They also recognise that happiness serves as both means and end. Happy children, growing in their understanding of what happiness is, will seize their educational opportunities with delight, and they will contribute to the happiness of others. (2003: 261)

Education in its widest sense

In the previous quotation, Noddings identifies education as happening both in school and at home. Such a wider understanding of education was identified in Scotland in the 1964 Kilbrandon Report into how to best deal with children in trouble. Kilbrandon argued for a model of social education: education in its widest sense, 'to include all children whose educational requirements are not met by the normal educational processes of the home or school' (para 244). This notion of social education was equated with 'upbringing', involving the various dimensions highlighted in other chapters of this volume.

Social pedagogy, similarly, stresses a conception of education in its widest sense, involving head, heart and hands, and incorporating cognitive, practical and affective strands. Perhaps not surprisingly, when academic education is considered within a holistic understanding of education in its widest sense, then attainments are better. Qualification levels for children from care settings from across Europe bear comparison with those of the general population (Petrie et al, 2006), which is manifestly not the case in the UK. Residential care holds out the possibility, then, to be an environment that promotes a culture of achievement. If residential child care is to become a learning environment in the widest sense, then those adults who work there need to think about their role in providing opportunities for children to learn and to enjoy. This can happen in all aspects of everyday living. Such a holistic and purposive approach to education has been clearly demonstrated with residential boarding schools for the elite worldwide. There has been ideological resistance to making such connections in the context of residential child care. These, perhaps, ought to be revisited.

An educationally rich residential child care

We are increasingly aware that learning is a social rather than just, or even primarily, an individual cognitive process. It happens in groups, or at the very least through relationships. While most Western psychological theory focuses on individual developmental processes, the Russian psychologist Vygotsky, whose work is becoming increasingly influential, claims that development takes place firstly on a social plane before it is subsequently incorporated into an individual's cognitive schema. Knowledge and meaning are socially constructed by those parties involved in the learning process – both teachers and learners – rather than being merely transmitted from one to the other, as more traditional views of teaching might suggest (Stremmel, 1993).

A central theme in Vygotsky's work relates to what he called the 'zone of proximal development' (ZPD). Essentially, children grow and can be supported in their growth towards the next stage of development through the guidance of appropriate adults or more skilled peers. The ZPD is socially mediated and formed through dialogue and relationship. Adults are accorded a role as 'more knowledgeable others' in working with children, to help them identify and develop their skills in particular areas. Likewise, peers can play a role in mediating this development, especially social development (Emond, 2000).

The identification of learning as a social process supported through relationships with more expert adults or peers makes Vygotsky's thinking particularly appropriate in residential child care practice. Such a perspective lends itself to working with groups because it is fundamentally social and broadly educational, rather than individual and problem-focused. It also signals the importance of relationships established between children and the adults with whom they work. Vygotsky thus provides a robust psychological underpinning to models of social education or social pedagogy. In many respects, residential child care needs to be first and foremost a place of social learning.

Drawing, implicitly, on Vygotsky's idea of the ZPD, Eichsteller and Holthoff (2010) conceptualise learning as taking place when learners can leave their comfort zone to explore the next level out in their environment. This they identify as the learning zone, where children and young people are forced to consider and extend the limits of their abilities. Pushed too far, they enter the panic zone, where their lack of knowledge and understanding and resultant anxiety inhibits their ability to learn. The aim for residential child care is continually to encourage children to step out of their comfort zones and into their learning zones.

To create opportunities where young people can encounter such learning opportunities, a degree of safety and trust must be present, and the level of challenge with which they are presented must provide a manageable fit with how they view themselves. This is where ideas such as the ZPD become meaningful in practice. Workers need to be able to arrange experiences and events that provide the correct amount of challenge and offer opportunities in a way that allow children and young people to achieve incrementally and at an appropriate pace and level. Experiences of achievement thus become a real platform for further success. As Powis et al note, 'One finds that a child who is unconfident in all areas of his life may need just one area of achievement from which he gains self-confidence and this can change his attitude to and performance in all the other areas' (1989).

Residential child care workers can help children in their care explore opportunities where learning does not have to be a painful or frustrating experience. From such a perspective, carers should begin with what really interests the young person and how they can build on those interests to create realistic learning opportunities through daily living activities. Many young people respond to personal coaching activities from a carer with whom they feel engaged. This highlights the importance of residential child care workers proactively engaging with each child or young person and not waiting for them to make the first move. In the absence of this element of intentionality on the part of staff, negative cultures can emerge that do not sufficiently value education. Learning to enjoy and achieve begins through relationships that matter, and where enjoyment and achievement are not rigid expectations but a natural consequence of these relationships.

Within such relationships encountered in the present, unencumbered by past feelings, young people find opportunities to experience themselves in new ways, which begin to weave together personal stories that include competence, mastery, trustworthiness, happiness and, perhaps most importantly, hope (Phelan, 2001b). Communication at these moments occurs through the senses and through shared experience, rather than simply through words. Experienced care workers might think about times they have engaged alongside young people in arduous physical activity, such as a long cycle ride or a challenging hill walk. Communication in many of these situations is non-verbal, based around presence, relationship, and 'doing with'. This shared experience can provide a powerful platform from which to identify and grasp what might be thought of as 'teachable moments' – the educational counterpart of the lifespace intervention. The central premise of a lifespace orientation is that 'the other 23 hours' are every bit as important as any more formal treatment. In an educational sense, the 24 hour curriculum – whereby an educational focus is maintained beyond the formal classroom experience – becomes a powerful driver for learning. It is increasingly evidenced that poorer children's educational attainments fall off and they fall behind their peers during school holiday periods rather than during term time (Alexander et al, 2001). It, therefore, behoves residential child care to be concerned with providing opportunities for learning throughout the children's stay and not to think of it as something that only happens during term time.

Creativity

Children who struggle with more traditional educational experiences may well have aptitudes that can emerge in more creative ways. All children ought to have access to the creative arts. They should have 'opportunities to enjoy beauty and creativity, and discover wonder' (Petrie and Chambers, 2009: 3). Specifically, children should be encouraged to read for enjoyment and some local authorities have taken steps to encourage this at an organisational level through the appointment of a Reading Champion (Linnane, 2008). Storytelling can provide an engaging point of entry to reading and literacy (Stevens et al, 2008). Children, generally also love the experience of going to a well-chosen play at the theatre. The experience of Camphill schools, which draw upon a range of creative activities in their work with children, might suggest that making music of some sort is accessible and enjoyable for all children and adults, irrespective of their level of ability. Most children love music and ought to at least have access to guitars and keyboards to rehearse their dreams of becoming rock stars.

Children in care should also have the opportunity to try out different types of food and, within reason, to eat out in different restaurants. Holidays should not merely be about keeping children entertained but should seek to introduce them to different ways of learning, thinking about and engaging in their worlds. A sense of history may also be invaluable in helping children understand their place in the world. There is a lack of training for residential workers in the UK to recognise the importance of such cultural activities or to provide them with the skills to do so. Again, there is a contrast between this situation and that in social pedagogical traditions where 'Music, drama, dance and the visual arts open [student pedagogues'] eyes to wider dimensions of existence and richer possibilities for the children they will work with' (Petrie and Chambers, 2009: 3).

The role of teachers and carers

As education has become entrenched in more instrumental and narrowly curriculum-based activities, the risk is that the role of the teacher is redefined and reduced to technique, with teachers as little more than technicians (Dunne, 1993). But teaching (and by this we include all teaching, not just classroom teaching) cannot be reduced to mere technique. This diminishes the centrality of the relational and artistic elements of good teaching. We have already noted that children achieve best when they enjoy what they are doing. An essential feature in their achievement involves their relationships with those around them. Children will learn best from someone they enjoy learning from (Glasser, 1998).

Curricular content may be pitched at the right level, but if it is not seen as relevant or made interesting – and if the teacher is not liked by the learner –it is unlikely that children will take much from it. As Palmer says, 'In our rush to reform education, we have forgotten a simple truth: reform will never be achieved by renewing appropriations, restructuring schools, re-writing curricula and revising texts if we continue to demean and dishearten the human resource called the teacher ...' (1998: 3). It is a central tenet of child and youth care that relationships count; the singer is every bit as important as the song when it comes to helping children enjoy and achieve. This applies to parents, preschool teachers, teachers and residential child care workers. Children learn best from those who catch their imagination and connect with them at a very personal level. This is a two-way process. Noddings observes that 'Clearly, if children are to be happy in schools, their teachers should also be happy. Too often we forget this obvious connection.' (2003: 261).

Noddings' argument identifies teaching as essentially relational and interactive rather than didactic and instructional. In social pedagogical terms, while it may not always be possible to teach, 'it is possible to create situations wherein it is impossible not to learn' (Eichsteller and Holthoff, 2010: 54). Learning is more likely when teachers or carers can demonstrate a sense of curiosity and openness in respect of their subject matter, as this can be infectious. When workers remain curious and comfortable in the uncertainty of not knowing everything then they can invite children to explore a topic or a problem with them. Freire (1972) provides a model of the teacher and student coming together to learn from one another and thereby to co-create understandings.

Adults who take an active role in children's education are implicated in their improved life chances. Jackson and Martin (1998) identified the presence of at least one adult who took a special interest in them and believed in them as being central to young people's successful transitions from the care system. Elements of belief and expectation are vital. If we expect children to continue to develop, grow, and achieve – whatever their disadvantages – they will do so (Palmer, 1998). When children do achieve particular things there should be some formal celebration of these, such as a special treat, or even something as small as a card or a favourite meal. However, adults can also acknowledge achievement in what White (2008) calls the common things of life, such as everyday rituals like high fives or pats on the back. These should be geared towards providing encouragement that is sincere, while also, on occasion, pointing out how things might be done better or differently. Small gestures of thanks or appreciation can foster a sense of achievement and self-worth.

There is a strong correlation between the educational achievements of parents and those of their children, with children performing significantly better educationally if their parents are university educated (Sutton Trust, 2010). In foster care, carers who had higher educational qualifications themselves almost invariably gave education top priority (Jackson et al, 2005). This fact ought to raise important political and professional messages for residential child care practice, where the majority of staff have never experienced tertiary education and thus are less likely to instil expectations in children in care about going on to university. There is another problem with the way that residential child care workers are currently educated. There is little in social work training, whether at professional or vocational levels, that actually equips care workers for providing children with opportunities for enjoyment or achievement. Social work training very often operates from a deficit model, where the focus is on children's problems. This can encourage risk-averse and overly proceduralised ways of interacting. Carers are not provided with the skills to coach a group of young footballers, to tie a fly for a fishing trip, to distinguish between a heron and a falcon, or to make Christmas decorations. If residential child care workers can do these things it is because, by chance, they bring such skills from other areas of their lives. Yet these are the very skills that help create an environment where children can achieve and have fun in so doing.

Humour

If enjoyment is central to achievement then residential child care ought to provide ready opportunities for such. Anyone who has worked in such settings will realise that opportunities for laughter are immense. But laughter is rarely factored into the way workers are conditioned to think about care. When laughter is acknowledged it can be subject to a suspicion that someone is being laughed at. For the most part this misunderstands the place of laughter in daily life of caring and contributes to a sterility in the experiences of residential care. It is through laughter that children learn about fun. Emond (2004) identifies how humour – expressed through wind-ups, acting up or teasing – plays a key role in group cohesion. Similarly, White notes that the 'opportunity for laughter and humour allows children to cope with mistakes, difference, the vagaries of language and culture, misfortune, stress and tension' (2008: 153–4). Furthermore, 'children who genuinely see the funny side of life find relationships easier than those who don't' (White, 2008: 154–5). In contexts where humour is employed appropriately – the use of nicknames, for instance – it might be seen as healthy and might speak of a connection and fondness between different parties in a relationship. Humour is thus fundamental to care. Digney suggests that 'humour makes it possible to let young people see that you care. Sharing a laugh, for example, can offer a non-threatening demonstration of empathy and caring. It is often easier for a young person to accept that someone cares about them if it is not explicitly stated but presented in a humorous manner' (2005: 12).

Summary

A number of important factors contribute to residential child care workers helping to create learning environments where children and young people can find opportunities to enjoy learning and begin achieving much more to their potential. Care workers play a central role in arranging and supporting learning experiences. In practice, residential child care involves making full use of a range of activities through which opportunities are provided for relationship building, the development of life skills and social competencies, as well as for experiencing fun. Think of how much time workers spend in their duty offices and compare the outcomes achieved there with what happens when young people and their carers engage in educationally rich learning experiences. The role of the carer involves getting involved in purposeful relationships with children and young people, not simply supervising them. The best supervision is achieved through participation with children and young people. In so doing, carers earn the respect of those with whom they work. There is much to be said for actively seeking opportunities to celebrate achievements – little achievements, big achievements and even quiet, very personal achievements. Humour can be a joyous way of celebrating relationships and helping to transform residential child care into positive growth experiences for young people and carers. It is only when we begin to think of education in such a wide, joyous and potentially liberating way that we can start to seriously address questions of educational underachievement in the care system.

Returning to the scenario

A number of things are going on here that create the opportunities for learning in a fun context. There are contextual factors that make learning more likely. The staff group includes both teachers and care workers who have come together to organise a group holiday in what might be thought of nowadays as an example of interdisciplinary or team working. They have also put themselves in a situation where a range of possible risks might be identified – from road accidents to group misbehaviour – and might in some cases be used as a reason to curtail activities. Many of these risks, however, can be minimised through a degree of planning and good group relationships.

There is some intentionality involved in creating the conditions for learning. The staff members involved knew that fishing might be a likely activity, so had packed in anticipation of this. After a few days involved in the shared activity of cycling around the countryside and living together, the group has bonded and is comfortable and can share jokes together. A sense of playfulness is apparent. Mr Turnbull is able to feed into this group dynamic to introduce his 'kipper' challenge. He knows Brendan and his interests and may have a notion that he will come back at him. He is able then to use Brendan's response to create what is called in the literature a teachable moment: an opportunity that must be sensed and seized by the teacher, and through which he or she has the chance to offer insight to his or her students. It might be thought of as the teaching counterpart of the lifespace intervention.

This teaching moment is maximised through the nature of the relationship that obviously exists between Mr Turnbull, Brendan and the rest of the group. Such relationships are developed through sharing the lifespace and through an element of shared history, by which actors in any scenario come to know each other's likes, interests and likely responses to situations. In such circumstances the use of nicknames, rather than being disrespectful, can become a healthy feature of relationships. Humour is a central element of the interaction – it is central to the interaction between Bernard and Mr Turnbull, but extends from this to include the whole group of staff and children. And through this use of humour the whole group learns what a kipper is.

Thoughts for practice

The essence of helping children to achieve and enjoy is to develop a culture that promotes these qualities. In current day parlance, this might be thought of as a learning organisation, where a spirit of learning permeates every aspect of the life of an organisation. At a basic level, staff should strive to make reading among children part of the culture of a home, through having books available, telling bedtime stories to younger (or older) children, taking children to the public library, identifying and sharing books they might like and engaging in discussion about reading.

Newspapers give children access to what is going on in the wider world. Make sure there are newspapers lying around and encourage children to read them, even if it's just the sports pages to start with. Encourage curiosity – don't close down questions. Use newspaper articles or television stories to engage in discussion about topical issues.

Take an interest in children's schoolwork, particularly any homework they might get. Getting children to engage with homework might be encouraged if staff members too are engaged in further study. If young people see staff studying and can recognise the hard work and frustrations but also the sense of achievement that go along with this, they are more likely to see learning as an ongoing and important part of life.

Think about what the learning opportunities might be when you organise activities and make sure you point them out to children as they encounter them. Make new opportunities and experiences available – lift your sights and those of the children.

Think about the ZPD and choose activities that will provide an appropriate challenge to children, those that are pitched just beyond their current level of competence but not beyond their capabilities.

Do things *with* children – when you do things alongside children or young people, things work a whole lot better. Staff participating in activities will often encourage children's involvement, and can strengthen and deepen relationships. These relationships are a powerful catalyst for further learning.

Find out what children like to do and encourage these interests through accessing suitable community groups and resources for them to pursue such activities. Introduce children to your own interests. When carers are enthusiastic about an activity this is likely to rub off on children.

Have fun – a light and humorous approach will more likely yield positive results. Be playful, laugh, laugh at yourself and delight in the fun. Offer genuine praise (children can pick up when it's not genuine). Make 'Well done' a part of your everyday vocabulary.

Give due regard in the recruitment process to employ care staff who place a high regard on education. In a similar vein, take account of the range of different interests and skills prospective staff have to offer. Adults who can engage with children across a range of learning experiences are likely to make the most rounded and effective care workers.

Further reading

Again, Nel Noddings' work is relevant. Her wider body of educational thinking is summarised and referenced at: www.infed.org/thinkers/noddings.htm

Kiaras Gharabaghi makes an important argument that residential child care ought to be based around a broad idea of education rather than treatment:Gharabaghi, K. (2012) 'Translating evidence into practice: supporting the school performance of young people living in residential group care in Ontario', *Children and Youth Services Review*, doi:10.1016/j. childyouth.2012.01.038.

The report of the YiPPEE project, which considers the pathways to further and higher education in young people from a public care background across five European countries is available at:

http://tcru.ioe.ac.uk/yippee/Portals/1/Final%20Report%20of%20the%20 YiPPEE%20Project%20-%20WP12%20Mar11.pdf

6

Active: a sense of purpose

Scenario

Jane is 10, an only child, born to a white mother and a father of African–Caribbean heritage. She was removed from her mother's care five years ago and has since been in a succession of foster placements and primary schools. She has never known her father, and prior to being taken into care she experienced neglectful and erratic care by her mother, who had relationship and addiction problems. Previous placements broke down due to schools and carers not being able to manage Jane's outbursts of temper and defiance. Psychologists have assessed Jane as having attention deficit hyperactivity disorder (ADHD) and attachment problems. She has difficulty focusing her conversation, is indiscriminate in attaching herself to adults and, as a result of her domineering attitude and aggression, she struggles to sustain friendships. She is underachieving in her schoolwork due to difficulties with concentration. Jane is now three months into a residential school placement, where her behaviour is challenging. However, she is also beginning to show some really endearing qualities and can be friendly and caring towards others.

The residential worker, John, aware of Jane's love of music and singing, has organised a karaoke evening where Jane has a microphone and is making a video of herself accompanying her favourite band. John has planned the session to end with him conducting an 'on the sofa' interview with Jane, pretending that she is an international star on tour. He hopes that handing the microphone back and forth during the mock interview will help Jane focus on the conversation and practise turn-taking within it.

Jane gives a rousing version of the band's latest single with her own choreography. She comes over to the sofa with John, who compliments her on her performance and begins the pretend interview.

John (playfully extrovert): "Jane, that was a fantastic performance! How long did it take you to learn the words of the song?" (He hands the mike to Jane and through the following exchange the mike gets handed back and forth.)

Jane: "About three weeks."

John: "Amazing, and how long have you been interested in the band?"

Jane: "I've been interested in the band all my life and I want my mum to take me to their next concert."

Jane's introduction of her mother to the conversation is unexpected and requires John to think on his feet as to how best to respond to this turn of events without foreclosing the connection he has made with Jane.

John: "So you would love to go to a concert with your mum?"

Jane (into the mike): "Yes." (nods)

John: "Tell me, Jane, how long is it since you saw your mum?"

Jane: "Five years …" (pauses and stares up to the ceiling) "… I think."

John: "Sounds like you still miss seeing your mum."

Jane (very calmly and clearly): "I do miss my mum and I don't really know why I am here."

John: "So you wish things could have been different for you and your mum."

Jane: "Yes."

The conversation continues for another 20 minutes. Jane occasionally gets distracted and loses focus. Mostly, however, she talks about her experiences in her last school and with her last carers. Initially she says everything had been wonderful and that she had little understanding of the reason for her move to residential school. With gentle direction and questioning from John, though, she speaks openly of the difficulties and upsets she experienced in her previous placements.

    The conversation concludes with Jane talking about some of the things that could get better for her in this new residential school. Her major hopes are to get better at her schoolwork and to make friends. John acknowledges how tough things have been for Jane and her sadness about not having a mum around who could do things with her. He finishes by saying he would like to help Jane get better at her work and make friends. He says he would like to talk further with her sometime about how these two things might happen.

Introduction

This chapter focuses on the purposeful use of activities as a central feature and a source of strength in residential child care. Like other authors of his time, Hungarian Holocaust survivor Eugene Heimler spent a lifetime writing about what he had learned through experiences as a teenager surviving two concentration camps for political prisoners and two extermination camps, including Auschwitz, where those entering the camp passed under a sign reading 'Work will set you free' (Heimler, 1975). As a teenager, Heimler found himself the principal carer of children working in the camp kitchens, supervising the peeling of potatoes and helping with the preparation of food for the guards. Through access to potato peelings and scraps of food, Heimler and some of these children survived and later resettled in the West.

Like other survivors, Heimler later wrote about psychological experiments involving meaningless work carried out with prisoners. When rubble caused by Allied Forces bombing needed to be cleared, volunteers stepped forward from among the prisoners to help clear it. Such activity had a purpose and gave prisoners a form of meaning in life. The Nazi psychologists decided to test the effects of 'meaningless work', requiring prisoners to move rubble from one end of the compound and then move it back again, hour after hour. As exhausted prisoners lost all sense of purpose, time and time again they either committed suicide by throwing themselves upon the electrified fences or were shot while trying to run away.

In his later professional work with chronically unemployed and so-called 'work-shy' youths, Heimler wrote about the emotional significance of purposeful activity. Purposeful activity is important for children or young people in helping general learning and in the development of a sense of personal wellbeing. Yet, for a number of reasons, the central role that activity plays in residential child care is often undervalued. Activities can be considered as little more than a time-filler – something to keep children occupied and to get adults through a shift. In many settings, funds set aside for activities can be handed over to children to do their own thing in the community, under a belief that this is providing them with normalising experiences. Activities available in-house can be limited to computer games or watching television. Money provided for activities is often spent on trips to the cinema, where staff and children hardly need to interact. That is not to suggest that allowing young people funds to meet up and hang about with friends is not important, or that commonplace activities such as the video game or the TV are to be discouraged; they can be productive if staff are aware of the opportunities these present to open up dialogue and to tap into experiences that might support children and young people's development. This, however, takes some forethought and intentionality on the part of the worker and sensitivity to the conversational cues that might emerge.

One of the reasons that the important role activities play in working with children and youths can be devalued might be a Poor Law legacy of less eligibility, discussed in Chapter One. There is a lingering assumption that state welfare provision should not be fun but should be about doing work. The 'work' involved in residential child care is often encompassed within care planning processes. Much care planning in residential child care seems to focus on some aspect of children's social, emotional or cognitive deficits. Against such a backdrop it can be difficult to consider that something like play might also be 'work', in the sense that it furthers the task of helping children grow and develop. A combination of the spectre of less eligibility and the failure to appreciate the central role of play and activities in normal child development can lead to them being used in some settings as a privilege to be withdrawn as a result of bad behaviour. An equally valid argument might be made that children who misbehave should be engaged in additional activities.

Another related reason that activities do not receive the prominence they should is, as we noted in the previous chapter, that training for social work or social care rarely includes any input on the importance of activities; nor does it equip residential workers with the skills that might be useful in incorporating these more systematically within their daily work. This is in contrast to the situation in social pedagogy, where up to a third of the curriculum is focused upon teaching students practical, cultural and recreational activities that they might utilise in their work. In the absence of specific training around activities, care workers are left to stand or fall on the basis of what they might bring to their work from their personal skills or interests.

Despite dominant conceptions of what seemingly 'professional' work might be, those who have worked for any length of time in residential child care will likely reflect that their most memorable or 'breakthrough' moments happened during some activity rather than in the course of some more formal counselling session. Phelan captures this tension between work and play when he speaks of working with children and young people as:

> connecting kids with their world ... to the universal things they
> will find in life which are available to us all – fun, games, sea sport,
> mountains, walks ... and ideas and knowledge. Is it possibly a sign of
> our own tendency to expect the worst that we offer all these cliché
> skills to problem children – conflict-resolution, problem-solving,
> anger-management, self-defence? ... I wonder how necessary these
> things would be if we offered them experience in sailing, vegetable
> growing, soccer, playing bongo drums or fixing bikes. (2001a: 1)

Programmes based around this latter type of activities would be truly strength rather than deficit focused.

The importance of play

Play is widely recognised as a powerful vehicle for learning and development. It sparks qualities of imagination and creativity and skills of turn-taking, and hence promotes both cognitive and social growth. The nature of play changes with age and stage. It need not all be formally organised. The kind of seemingly aimless 'mucking about' and horseplay in which teenagers engage can be just as important in helping them come to a sense of their place in the world as is toddlers' play with bricks. Although often discouraged within child protection discourses, horseplay can be a natural part of growing up, for many boys in particular. Biddulph (2003) suggests that to get along with boys one should learn to wrestle. While needing to be aware of some of the issues that could arise as a result of physical play and to acknowledge that different members of staff might have different comfort levels in engaging in such activity, we should avoid pathologising what, for many children, are normal developmental behaviours. The concerns that have built up around physical touch within the child protection dominated UK practice cultures are not shared in other countries. In Denmark, for instance, Andersen (2009) refers to the existence of a 'tumbling room' in a residential community, where controlled 'tussles' with other residents and staff allow boys to develop a realistic measure of their own capacities.

Types of play and activity

Acknowledging the importance of play in childhood, Altman (2002) argues that good child and youth care practice needs to include an understanding of the meanings that play might have and its intrinsic value in such work. He also notes that through observing children at play, care workers can identify personality and character traits that may prove valuable in constructing particular interventions with them. The range of activities available to workers and children in residential child care is almost endless. It can include:

> expressive arts; skill development (manual dexterity, use of tools, etc.); music; singing; drama and stage production; dance and movement; sports and exercise; physical relaxation activity; emotional discovery games; group games; individual projects; cooperative games; outdoor and wilderness activities; photography, videotape, audio activity,

cooking, carpentry, construction, exploration and discovery activity, and role playing and simulations. (Phelan, 2001a: 5)

Putting on a play or a pantomime can offer opportunities in acting, lighting, stage construction, making props and clothing. Without stereotyping or excluding, there may be arguments for arranging different activities for boys and girls. The Gender Equality Duty (see Children in Scotland, 2008) recognises that boys and girls may have different needs and places an obligation on services to respond to these differentially; activity programming may be one area where it is appropriate to do so.

The benefits of purposeful activity

There are many life skills to be learned and much enjoyment to be gained through individual recreation and leisure activities, and also from team sports and competitions. Being active, feeling active, thinking active and living active all help to reinforce personal health and wellbeing. There is a growing body of research showing that participation in activities, hobbies and useful tasks promotes resilience (MacLean, 2003). Likewise Steckley (2005), in her study of the role of the school football team in a residential school, identifies the resilience-promoting possibilities of purposeful activity, while also highlighting the potential of team sport in fostering pro-social behaviour and a sense of belonging. VanderVen (1999) highlights the opportunities provided by an organised jog to encourage staying power on the part of children. White suggests that sport allows the opportunity for children (and adults) to rehearse skills needed to operate in everyday life, such as 'boundaries, self-expression and training, teamwork, the acceptance of losing and winning, and playing in a defined space and way' (2008: 170). He also acknowledges, though, that not all children are adept at nor interested in sport. Social skills can equally be learned and practised through a whole range of activities. 'Stickability', for instance, might be fostered through perseverance in the fine motor skills required in activities such as jewellery making or extended board games, while the importance of teamwork is as apparent in playing in a music group or performing a drama production as it is in team sports.

Pitching activities at the right level

Residential care workers need to exercise some judgement about the level at which to pitch activities. If a chosen activity is too onerous in respect of the physical, cognitive or fine motor demands it places on a child, such an activity may reinforce a sense of learned helplessness (Seligman, 1992), whereby past experiences of feeling unable to do things may carry through into subsequent activities. On the other hand, if an activity is too easy it can lead to boredom and is unlikely to promote further learning. The trick is to identify activities that push children to the next level of their abilities. In this sense, Vygotsky's idea of the zone of proximal development (ZPD) discussed in the previous chapter might also have a resonance with activity programming. The ZPD can be best reached through the involvement of more expert others, whether adults or peers, in 'scaffolding' children's learning towards the next level. Carers might think about playing a game such as table tennis or pool. If you play against someone far better than you the likely outcome is discouragement. By the same token, playing someone who is much less able can be frustrating and boring. Your game is likely to improve when you play someone just a little bit more proficient than you. In other areas of activity, children might learn incrementally more sophisticated skills in model making, for instance, or art. This calls for a level of intentionality on the part of workers when initiating activities and pitching them at the right level for participants. VanderVen (1999) draws on learning theory to propose an apprenticeship or situated learning model whereby children move from participating on the periphery of an activity to becoming full participants.

Time, space and activity

The type of activities that might be possible in a particular care home can be promoted or restricted by a number of organisational variables, including size, space, and the way in which time is utilised. Working on the assumption that activities are something to be encouraged in the life of a home, some thought should be given to considering how such variables act to encourage or inhibit activities. At a simple level, the size of a centre can have a major impact on the kind of activities that can take place in it. School football teams, as discussed above, are probably only options within residential schools, although smaller children's homes might manage to muster a five-a-side team comprising residents and staff. Children wanting to play team sports might have to be encouraged and supported to access these in the community. Indeed, children and young people should be encouraged to engage in social activities in the community, from football teams through organised groups such as Scouts or Guides, to drama groups and music lessons. These, though, should complement rather than substitute for involvement in the everyday activities that present in residential care.

Use of time

The staff rota largely determines the use of time in a residential centre. A number of factors feed into the construction of rotas, most of which are based around perceived economic efficiency or staff preferences. Rarely does the management of the rota take account of its impact on activity programming. In fact, more often than not standard rota patterns – consisting of early and late shifts – can cut across much activity planning by placing demands on staff either to leave or to begin a shift in the middle of the afternoon. Such requirements mean that without advance planning and staff commitment to be flexible in their hours of work, activities like extended or impromptu day trips become more problematic. Strict adherence to set shift patterns can lead to a lack of purposeful activity in some staff groups. Such cultures may be reinforced in situations where agencies have to rely on temporary staff to fill their rota.

Use of space

Henry Maier (1982) wrote about how the spaces we create in residential child care tend to control us and influence our actions. So, rather than being controlled by the spaces in which they work, carers need to make conscious use of all the spaces and facilities available for use in their home or residence. In exploring activities that might be nurtured in residential settings, imagine walking through the residence as a child or young person. Enter different rooms and spaces, pausing to reflect on activities that commonly happen in these places; different rooms and spaces afford different possibilities.

Activities that happen in kitchens and dining rooms

Food reaches to the hearts of most children and young people and is at the centre of developing nurturing relationships between adults and children. This means that cooking and baking smells, warmth, cups of tea, coffee or juice and welcoming chat make the kitchen/dining room area a kind of 'mission control' centre for most residential child care centres. Invitations to be active around kitchens in support of resident group life and to nurture relationships through kitchen–related activities range from food preparation, cooking, baking, setting the table, cleaning up and dish washing. Carers can engage in kitchen-related tasks more positively if they think of them as activities that offer opportunities for engagement and learning rather than as chores. Preparing and cooking food also affords great opportunities to challenge gender stereotypes and perhaps, through cookery nights themed around different national cuisines, afford opportunities to stimulate discussion about other cultures. Mealtimes themselves provide fertile ground for developing social skills, especially when staff sit and eat alongside children and can model the appropriate use of cutlery and the development of relaxed after dinner social conversation, which can be crucial in the development of group norms and cultures.

Activities that happen in bedrooms

Bedrooms include learning opportunities associated with laundry, tidying up clothes, perhaps ironing, making the bed, vacuuming the room, clearing rubbish bins, and so on. Once again, the issue isn't about simply introducing rules about household chores. Instead, carers can benefit from thinking about the nurturing opportunities for learning life skills. When life skills are learned interactively with a sensitive carer, relationship building and task-oriented learning go hand in hand. Bedrooms offer opportunities for children and young people to get private space to read or listen to music. They also afford opportunities for one-to-one time with workers; for example, in reading a younger child a bedtime story.

Activities that happen in public spaces

Most residential centres have public spaces where everyone gathers, often to watch television, perhaps listen to music, watch DVDs, play computer games or even to attend weekly house meetings. Unlike private spaces where the occupant sets most of the rules about entry and use of facilities, in public spaces of a residence there are more frequently ground rules. Caution needs to be exercised around designated chairs or seating arrangements in the public spaces of any residential child care facility. Young people persistently identify their own personal seating spaces and it follows that group dynamics will often feature prominently around seating arrangements with the arrival and departure of residents. Ground rules will normally apply with regard to the television or video controller(s) and sometimes include unwritten rules such as 'we always watch this programme'. Sports fans frequently book their seats for the big game, while reality shows are likely to be as central a feature of the life of residential homes as they are in many families.

Many opportunities will present themselves daily to engage in shared activities in family rooms and sitting rooms. The availability of a range of board games or art and construction materials provides opportunities for social learning experiences and skills development. Availability of video cameras to encourage drama and film making by children and young people can also encourage skill development, and through role play, for example, creates opportunities for children and young people to 'step outside' their own experience of the world. The learning of social repartee represents an important set of life skills. Creating special times around television, DVDs and particular sports events presents valuable opportunities for children and young people to feel included and valued.

Activities that happen in grounds and gardens

Moving outside the home, one commonly encounters a deck, patio and gardens. Gardens may range from the postage stamp variety to vast expanses of greenery, foliage and play areas. Add the prospect of a pet or pets – ranging from goldfish to horses – depending on the size of the place, and a whole new world of opportunities might be opened for a child or young person. Decks and patios offer the opportunity to engage young people in barbecues and picnics. If there is space, gardens can be used for kicking a ball or playing games like badminton, tether ball or throwing a ball with the dog. Growing plants of different types in gardens or window boxes might offer up numerous opportunities to encourage a sense of care and nurture around themes of feeding, caring and growing. Children or young people who have never had access to decks, patios or gardens are sometimes more hesitant. Most, however, come to enjoy such public spaces that offer opportunities for both private and public activities. Playing in a big garden is a terrific experience for children of all ages, involving important life skills.

Pacing activities

Some activities are better engaged with at particular times of the day and some thought should be given to changing the pace of activities over the course of the day. In the mornings, at least during school term, there ought to be a sense of purpose apparent in ensuring that children get ready and get into the right mood for school. At other points in the day, and depending on age and stage, a cartoon DVD might encourage imagination and animated activity, going out for an ice cream might help change mood, an iPod music session might facilitate restorative 'alone time' or five-a-side football could nurture relational group work. Physical activities, though, should be brought to a close in sufficient time to allow a slowing down before bedtime. VanderVen (2003) identifies the different types of activities such as a bath and/or a bedtime story that can be used at the end of a day to help this 'slowing down' process. Bedtime routines tailored to individual children's ages and stages can provide fantastic opportunities for individual time, nurture and, if it involves reading a book, discussion around some of the themes that might be raised in children's literature.

Activities and risk

Children and young people often engage in a variety of sporting, recreational and leisure activities. Loughmiller (1979) has long pointed out the educational and character-building opportunities offered by outdoor activities. Inevitably, some risk of injury attaches to children becoming involved in such activities. As a consequence, there has been a proliferation of guidance and prescription with regard to such activities. In a wider societal climate in which ideas of risk predominate, a number of misconceptions and myths have come to prevail, to the extent that 'fear of letting children play unsupervised is limiting children's freedom, to the detriment of their physical, mental and emotional well-being' (Gill, 2007: 1). A Danish contributor to an international conference, describing the adventure playground in the grounds of the residential centre where he was director, said that people often asked him if children got injured. He responded that they occasionally did but that better a broken arm than a broken psyche. Others were dumbfounded when the director of a Texas-based residential school spoke of young people engaging in rodeo bull riding. A ridiculous number of obstacles are placed in the way of staff wanting to engage in outdoor activities with children, such as requirements imposed by local authorities that they need prescribed outdoor education qualifications in order to take children for a low-level hike or for a paddle by the seaside. This particularly impedes spontaneity in responding to favourable weather conditions or specific requests. For child care workers, teachers and activity leaders the effect of a risk culture is compounded by the fear of being blamed should anything go wrong. It is understandable in a climate in which childhood is over-regulated that professionals and 'agencies may feel under pressure to accede to the demands of the most risk averse' (Gill, 2007: 3). The low status of child care as a profession, Gill (2010) argues, can make it more difficult for residential workers to resist the degree to which children in care settings are overprotected.

As stated by David Bell, former Chief Inspector of Schools in England, the reality is that 'the benefits of outdoor education are far too important to forfeit, and by far outweigh the risks of an accident occurring' (cited in Gill, 2010: 2). Obviously, staff need to take the reasonable precautions that any good parent would take when engaging in such activities; indeed, they have to be aware of their additional obligations to other people's children when organising activities for children in care. For this reason they are expected to carry out risk assessments before they engage in any activity. In actual fact there is an increasing realisation in the professional literature that the kinds of risk assessment that have emerged in response to such expectations are rarely useful or meaningful. Commentators rightly question 'how far have these actually met the needs of the situation or whether they may be a "smoke screen" to convince ourselves and others that we are doing something positive in a situation over which we have little control?' (Cree and Wallace, 2005: 126).

Of course, staff engaging in outdoor activities need to take sensible safety precautions: they need to have the correct equipment for the planned activity; they need to be aware of weather conditions; they need to know what route they might take and any possible hazards; they need to take basic steps to let people know where they are and to institute arrangements to maintain contact. What is at least as important as any procedural requirements, however, is the professional competence and authority of the staff members involved. Without basic relational skills and authority then risk assessment formats and the various consent forms that proliferate such areas of practice are of limited use. The Duke of Edinburgh Award Scheme's *Expedition guide* states that, of all the qualities entailed in the safety and wellbeing of participants completing their expeditions, 'that of sound judgement is the most important. Sound judgement, along with responsibility and maturity, arises from effective training coupled with progressive and varied experience over a period of time. It cannot develop unless there are opportunities to exercise judgement' (cited in Gill, 2010: 6). Merely following procedure cannot substitute for – and may in fact impede – the development of sound judgement of this sort.

Residential care workers as experience arrangers

Phelan suggests that 'the essential task of child and youth care work is to arrange experiences that promote a belief in competence and hope' (1999: 25). In making this case he argues that the primary strength of child and youth care does not rest upon 'verbal counselling strategies, therapeutic conversations held in an office or insight into past experiences' (Phelan, 1999: 25). Many of the children and families we work with in residential child care often find it difficult to engage in office-based therapies. Past life experiences converge to impose a particular life script – one that, although it may be self-defeating, is nevertheless well defended and resistant to the good intentions of some well-meaning social worker or residential worker seeking to bring these past experiences to the surface, often without any clear idea of what they might do next. The creation of conversations that emerge in a natural way, through purposeful activities, tends to be led by the child or family, and there is therefore greater motivation to engage – and indeed lead – the worker, rather than the other way round.

The role of activity and of the residential care worker as activity arranger is to introduce what Phelan (2001a) calls an experience gap, which puts a stutter into the self-defeating stories that hold children back, introducing the possibility that a different story – one that includes qualities of hope and competence – might begin to inform the way they think about their lives. Activities, therefore, need to be arranged in such a way that they begin to challenge perceptions of the self as hopeless or unworthy or omnipotent, and gradually to substitute such scripts with other possible ways of thinking and, ultimately, of being. Phelan (1999) notes that the development of a revised story does not come easily. A lengthy series of arranged experiences will be required in order to overturn entrenched personal narratives. The benefits of purposeful use of activity might, thus, be thought of as a process rather than a quick-fix event.

Relationships – the common third

The use of activity-based work with children and young people is not an instrumental task but a relational one. Workers are not objective and detached therapists within such a model but 'fellow travellers' (Phelan, 2001b). The social pedagogical idea of the 'common third', whereby the pedagogue and the young person share and have a joint claim on an activity in all of its different stages from idea to execution, captures this idea. Activity can allow the creation of a 'free space' 'where the usual rules of life don't have to exist' (Phelan, 2001b: 3). One might think of staff and children playing a computer game together, perhaps, and finding that particular children are more skilled than the staff, or a camping trip where the children are more adept at foraging for firewood than the workers who are accompanying them. Such situations create a dynamic where normal hierarchical relationships are turned on their head. A sense of equality and common purpose becomes apparent within relationships forged through shared involvement in activities. This can be carried forward into everyday life, where relationships become more relaxed, trusting and genuine, characterised by a greater reciprocity and respect.

One of the principles of a child and youth care approach as identified by Garfat and Fulcher (2011) is that workers ought to do 'with', not 'for' or 'to': this refers to how carers engage with children and young people, helping them to learn and develop through doing things together. This is especially important when children are capable of doing things themselves, even if under supervision (see, for example, Delano and Shah, 2011). Carers do not stand back ordering children or young people about but engage relationally, walking alongside them as a guide. This process of 'doing with' requires the carer's ongoing commitment to a reciprocating relationship between him or herself and the child or young person, monitoring the changing dimensions and experiences of that relationship. Whether it be in supervision, with a family, in a rural garden, or engaging in other activities, the focus of caring involves being and doing *with* a child or young person. This idea is perhaps summed up by Trieschman (1982), who claimed, 'When we do things to young people and not with them, it's not going to work so well.'

Summary

For too long, activities in residential child care have not been considered in sufficiently purposeful ways. Activities have been thought of in terms of keeping children and young people occupied, amused and entertained. At another level, ideas of normalisation have often led to children being left to their own devices. This fails to maximise the opportunities provided by activities for children to have fun, to develop a range of skills, and perhaps most importantly to build relationships with other children and with those adults who participate alongside them in activities. Relationships developed around shared activities are often more powerful and helpful than those based around more formalised interventions with children and young people.

There are many reasons or arguments that can be employed not to maximise the use of activities in the programmes of a home or school, from a lack of resources to the demands of health and safety or risk agendas. Most of these can be overcome with appropriate imagination on the part of workers and managers.

Returning to the scenario

Returning to the case scenario that introduces this chapter, we consider what might be going on to make this a meaningful activity for Jane. It is evident that John, in a relatively short time, has built up a trusting relationship with Jane and is able to respond sensitively to her. He has a sense, however sketchy this may be at this stage of a relationship, of Jane's family circumstances and of possible responses to issues of disrupted or disorganised attachment patterns (Howe, 1995).

Engaging responsively requires sensitive handling of opportunity events in the daily lives of children or young people. Paying attention to someone in a conversation or 'attending' is an important feature in any relationship. The worker is also careful and skilful in his use of language and his responses to Jane. He 'listens to and validates' (De Jong and Berg, 2002), acknowledging Jane's expression of sadness that her mother is not around for her. By repeating and paraphrasing what Jane has said, he allows her to take the next step in where the conversation goes and is respectful of her by not forcing the direction or pace of the conversation.

In building up a picture of Jane, John draws upon a cultural or sub-cultural awareness of the kind of bands that young girls might like. This kind of tacit knowledge allows the development of a relationship beachhead (Trieschman et al, 1969) that creates some element of common ground between Jane and John, or what the social pedagogic literature would call the 'common third'.

In thinking about the kind of activity to which she might respond, John has worked out that Jane has particular difficulties in social interaction and specifically in turn-taking. So he has constructed an activity that allows her to practise this. There is, thus, intentionality behind his intervention. He has constructed a playful and fun activity, through which Jane can build on her strengths and interests in pop music and singing, and through this develop her communication skills. In his actual engagement, he is mindful of Dan Hughes' (2006) concept of 'PLACE' (playful, loving, accepting, curious and empathic) as providing a guide for workers engaging with children and young people, particularly those who are more difficult to engage in conversation.

Jane unexpectedly invites the worker into her inner world of sadness that she does not have her mother in her life. This requires the worker to think on his feet. He is able to respond to the opportunity event that Jane's unexpected change of direction provides, to keep the channels of communication open and allow Jane to develop her train of thought and to process her feelings. He does so through continuing the mock interview. This becomes the medium for the developing conversation, thus shifting the focus of Jane talking about distressing issues in a more traditional counselling type situation to one that she experiences as less threatening, and where she is more in control.

As the interview progresses, the worker skilfully moves the focus of the interaction on from Jane's feelings of distress to a consideration of what might now be different. While this unexpected opportunity occurring within the lifespace may offer pointers suggesting future work with Jane, the most important point is that John has established a sense of connection and trust with Jane. She may or may not subsequently use this to begin to express strong emotions and feelings about her past and to think about the future. John has, at least, made himself available for future conversation should Jane choose to go down this road.

While activities might lead to therapeutic possibilities as in this case, this should not become the primary reason for engaging in activities. To consider activities only for what therapeutic benefit they might bring is perhaps to take life too seriously – activities have merit in their own right as providing fun and it is perhaps only when they are experienced as fun by children and adults that they become such an important arena for helping children grow and develop.

Thoughts for practice

The opportunities for carers to engage with children and young people in purposeful activity in residential child care settings are virtually endless. The key word or idea is 'purposeful'; this elevates what might be thought of as everyday and mundane to something that is replete with potential for enjoyment and learning. It requires carers to think more consciously and imaginatively about activities and the purpose they might serve.

Staff groups might think about setting up regular activities within the daily or weekly calendar – such as a jogging club, five-a-side football games, games nights or make-up or cooking nights – so that these become embedded within the culture of a home or school.

Think about activities that don't cost money but are sufficiently different to be attractive to children, such as, for example, games of tag in the park or night hikes.

Ensure that a home has a ready supply of equipment that might be used for activities, such as playing cards, board games, art and craft materials, books, a karaoke machine, footballs, musical instruments, bikes, camping gear, and so on.

It may be illuminating to look through care plans to consider what sort of issues are addressed and what kind of strategies are proposed to address these, as well as whether activities feature within children and young people's care plans. Consider whether particular skills might be developed through engagement in appropriately conceived activities.

Again, as a staff group, a worthwhile activity might be to consider how the physical layout of a building and the staff rota operate to enhance or inhibit opportunities for particular activities.

Encourage staff members to think about what their own interests and skills might be and how these might be shared with the children – if need be, try and facilitate staff developing these interests through further training.

Encourage staff to engage in activities alongside children rather than just supervising these.

Consider very carefully before withdrawing activities as a sanction. This is not to suggest that access to activities should be what Whittaker (1979) calls 'strings-free' – it may well not be appropriate to offer an enjoyable activity to a child who has been abusing staff all day, but neither is it appropriate to use activities as an easy sanction. Appropriately arranged activities may actually serve to bring a recalcitrant young person back on side.

Further reading

Karen VanderVen is perhaps the foremost writer on activities in child and youth care:

VanderVen, K. (2005) 'Transforming the milieu and lives through the power of activity: theory and practice', *Cyc-online*, no 82, www.cyc-net.org/cyc-online/cycol-1105-vanderven.html

Jack Phelan's paper on activities is helpful:

Phelan, J. (2001a) 'Another look at activities', *Journal of Child and Youth Care*, vol 14, no 2, pp 1–7, www.cyc-net.org/cyc-online/cycol-0107-phelan.html

The Scottish Institute for Residential Child Care has produced guidance on outdoor activities for staff in residential child care, debunking some of the health and safety assumptions that can inhibit activities:

Celcis (Centre for Excellence for Looked After Children in Scotland) (2010) 'Go outdoors: guidance and good practice on encouraging outdoor activities in residential care', www.celcis.org/resources/entry/go_outdoors_guidance_and_good_practice_on_encouraging_outdoor_activities

7

Respected and responsible: the idea of citizenship

Scenario

Jade is 15 and Mark is 14, both white. They are in the sitting room of a five bedroom adolescent unit located in a detached house in a residential suburb of a large city. Jane has been living there for four months and Mark has been there for just over two weeks. Two workers, Liz and Scott, are in the kitchen.

Jade is very overweight and has been making serious attempts to control her eating and take exercise. She can be very moody and volatile and there have been instances where she has needed to be physically restrained. She has hit out at other young people and at staff when she has lost her temper. She has been very remorseful after these incidents and has asked for help in controlling her temper and her anger. So far, most of Jade's anger appears when she is not able to express herself verbally and or when she perceives a threat from others.

Mark has so far maintained a very low profile and has been quiet in the house. He has a history of severe difficulties in school and is currently excluded for verbally abusing a teacher.

Liz and Scott hear raised voices and go through to investigate. They hear Mark's voice: "Yer ma."

Jade: "Naw, your ma."

Mark: "Naw, your ma. I shagged your ma last night – she's even fatter than you, you fat slag."

Jade (making her way aggressively towards Mark): "The only thing you shag is little boys, you gay boy."

Jade pushes Mark. He moves to go back towards Jade and looks like he is going to strike her. He sees the staff and moves aside. Jade lunges towards Mark. Liz and Scott believe she is about to hit out and take hold of her and physically restrain her with the techniques used in the organisation. Jade is screaming abuse at Mark and Mark leaves the room when asked to by staff. Jade turns her anger to the staff.

Jade (shouting at Scott): "What are you doing, you paedo? Is that all you can do, restrain little girls? You touched my bum, you paedo. You're in trouble, just wait and see."

Jade struggles violently for several minutes until, gradually, she responds to the staff and begins to calm down. Jane starts to cry as she calms and through sobs tells the staff that Mark had been winding her up and making negative comments about her weight all morning. She says that she tried to tell him to stop being abusive but the more she told him the more he said things. She said she was pushing him out of the way to leave the room when the staff came in.

Liz and Scott explain that they could only go on what they saw when they entered the room and they were sorry that they did not appreciate the whole picture. They apologise to Jade for having to take hold of her and explain that they were worried that someone was going to get hurt. They undertake to speak to Mark and talk through what Jade should do if Mark bullies her again.

Introduction

Respect, as a rule, is accorded to those who live respectable lives – people who conduct themselves with integrity and treat others, in turn, with high regard. In this regard, respect might be thought to be earned: by acting respectfully one receives the benefits of such action in return. Respect is the cornerstone of meaningful relatedness in our world – while definitions and expressions may change according to culture and context, the fundamental principle remains the same: how you are with others influences how they are with you. In this regard, respect is not just earned but is also learned, through experience. 'Children who are treated with love and respect come to believe they are persons of value. But those who feel unwanted or rejected neither respect themselves or others' (Brendtro and du Toit, 2005: 27). This chapter also addresses the issue of responsibility. It introduces ideas of 'respect-ability' and 'response-ability', emphasising the need to help children and young people develop abilities that are necessary for them to be respectable and responsible. The importance of appropriate adults in modelling the learning of new – or the unlearning of old – behaviours is also addressed. The lifespace is identified as the principal arena for developing and practising respectful and responsible behaviours.

Background

Historically, a central purpose in the use of residential child care was that of character development. This focus derived, largely, from the religious roots of care provision, most of which was operated by religious orders or religiously based charities. Houseparents were appointed to care settings on account of their standing as good Christian men and women. Nowadays, such explicitly religious motivations might be thought of as overly pious, narrow and rigid, and there is no doubt that Christian piety could often be expressed in fairly unchristian ways. Expectations centred on a rarely questioned, and not necessarily reciprocated or deserved, respect for adult authority.

Offending behaviour was thought to be indicative of bad character, and residential child care was often the first response to address what were perceived to be moral failings. The obvious response to this was a form of care where the predominant emphasis was on tight discipline and behaviour management.

The growth in psychological thinking, from the time of Freud in the 1920s onwards, shifted the focus of care from a religiously rooted concern for the soul to concern for the psyche (Smith, 2012). There is no doubt that one of the real advances in residential child care over recent decades has been a greater understanding of – and attention to – the psychological underpinnings of children's behaviours and the search for 'treatment' models to address these, rather than ascribing moral judgement. In reality, almost all children in residential care have had very disadvantaged and often abusive past experiences. As a consequence, many of their needs have remained unmet or inadequately met, with resultant behavioural manifestations.

However, the prominence given to 'treatment' models, allied with the decline in religion and a corresponding rise in secularism and moral relativism across society, has led to a situation where it has become more difficult for adults to focus on moral character in bringing up children. Adults can feel less confident in imposing their worldview upon children they care for, lest they be 're-traumatised'. Moreover, children are now decreed to have particular rights (which we discuss in Chapter Nine), and the kind of climate where adults could assert that they know best and make all the important decisions in children's care has become rather more tenuous and ambiguous. The kind of moral purpose that, for good or ill, was evident in religiously run residential care establishments has been superseded by a lack of certainty on the part of carers about what they can and cannot do in respect of children in their care (Webb, 2010).

The turn towards seeking psychologically informed understandings and interventions, and the shift in mindset towards taking children's views into account in providing care, are both welcome developments. However, carers also need to assert some wider moral purpose to care and to consider how they play an active role in shaping children's characters, rather than just being aware of their underlying emotional needs. Failure to take responsibility for doing so leaves children to their own devices in circumstances that often render them ill-equipped for a world beyond residential child care.

While government policy has stressed the importance of children's rights, it has simultaneously been presiding over increasingly punitive attitudes towards offending or 'anti-social' youths (Reeves, 2012). This is manifest in the growth of youth justice professionals with supposed expertise in dealing with offending behaviour. One of the consequences of this, however, is that youth justice 'experts' have allowed residential staff off the hook around dealing with offending in their everyday care of children. Care has been emptied of its necessary controlling and guiding dimensions.

Failure to address children's behaviour adequately is likely to have deleterious consequences for children as they come into contact with other parts of the system. Indulgent or insufficiently proactive parenting styles, which much of the care system appears to model, have a negative impact on children's learning and behaviour (Cameron and Maginn, 2008). Rod Morgan (2006), former head of the Youth Justice Board in England and Wales claims that many children end up in the criminal courts because teachers and care home workers have become afraid to discipline them for bad behaviour. In a similar vein, research into a fast-track children's hearings pilot scheme in Scotland (Hill et al, 2005) reveals that most of those children identified as persistent offenders achieved that status while in local authority care. Criminalisation as a direct consequence of being in care presents a real indictment of the care system. We should not accept the link between care and criminal careers without question (Taylor, 2006). However, to address the all too common linkage that does exist in many care settings, the system must begin to address questions of behaviour and character development that are rooted in a holistic understanding of children's needs, rather than just in a superficial understandings of their rights.

There are consequences for carers too of an extension of legalistic and contractual approaches to care. Fulcher and Ainsworth (2006) note that these render staff vulnerable to litigation or other legal action. This, in turn, frequently results in a primary – entirely understandable – concern on the part of staff for their own safety, resulting in a reluctance to engage in the more intimate or messy aspects of care. At a very practical level, the fear that staff might breach children's rights can be manifest in a failure to address misbehaviour. The 'you can't do that' culture that can develop in residential care is not merely evidence of children asserting a voice. It can also have the effect of disabling staff and inuring young people to the consequences of and responsibilities for their actions. But, of course, such a superficial view of rights does not extend to the criminal justice system once young people have left care.

The failure of residential child care, and indeed of schooling and other social service provision, to address children's behaviour in the context of their overall upbringing – combined with public and political concern about youth misbehaviour – might be implicated in an increasingly punitive turn in relation to young people. When adults do not feel sufficiently confident in addressing behaviour at a relational level, they often turn to systems. This has been evident in the expansion of secure accommodation over recent decades and the introduction of a range of measures around anti-social behaviour to address criminal and nuisance activities by young people.

There is much talk in the media and elsewhere about young people lacking respect and responsibility. The previous UK government even went so far as to appoint a 'respect tsar' in an attempt to ensure these qualities in everyday life. In schools there is a renewed interest in citizenship education, strands of which reflect this current societal focus on encouraging respect and responsibility. While few would argue against the qualities of respect and responsibility, in the current social climate ideas of responsibility can too readily 'responsibilise' children in ways that ascribe individual responsibility and fail to take sufficient account of social circumstances (Goldson, 2002). Responsibility, in this sense, is implicated in punitive youth justice agendas.

Most of this external focus on trying to impose respect and responsibility is misconceived because it resurrects the premise that such qualities are lacking due to moral culpability. It also assumes that children and young people are rational actors, making conscious decisions to misbehave and become involved in nuisance behaviour. From such perspectives, respect and responsibility simply require legislation and its rigorous enforcement. However, many children in care find it very difficult to act responsibly or respectfully because they have not learned or experienced respect or responsibility – they just seem to find themselves getting 'into bother' at times. In the words of a Native American proverb, 'Hurt people hurt people': the lack of respect and responsibility apparent in many young people has its roots in either bad experiences or an absence of good experiences of upbringing.

While policy and many professional assumptions might attempt to reduce the development of respect and responsibility to procedure and legalistic anti-social behaviour measures, the reality is that such qualities emerge through everyday experiences of care. Residential child care needs to provide the conditions that nurture respect and responsibility. According to Jones, if the state does not ensure children's moral development, then 'children cannot be blamed when their character remains under-developed' (2010: 23). This requires that the question of responsibility is considered through a different lens. It is not merely that children have to learn to be responsible, but that adults too have to assume responsibility for children and young people's upbringing. Care and education, according to Furedi, are in the first instance about the exercise of adult responsibility. Yet very often, and for understandable reasons, 'adults have become estranged from the task of taking responsibility for the younger generation' (2009: 3).

Rules-based approaches

The misconception that children and young people grow up good through the application of rules, policies or techniques has led residential child care to experiment with token economies, behavioural contracts, policies to address issues such as bullying, a range of proprietary programmes to address social skills or anger management and statements of legal rights with corresponding complaints procedures. While these may in some circumstances have a place, in terms of providing some guidance around social norms such prescriptions in themselves offer little towards helping children develop respect or responsibility. An over-reliance on systems also throws up its own practical difficulties. Rules often come to contradict one another and children, consciously or otherwise, expose and challenge such inconsistencies, thereby rendering a rule devalued and largely meaningless.

In seeking to understand and consider how best to respond to children and young people's behaviour, there is benefit in moving beyond psychological, legalistic or procedural considerations to incorporate, also, an awareness of philosophical perspectives. Rule and contract-based approaches to how people relate to one another are rooted in a particular ethical tradition commonly associated with the 18th century Prussian philosopher Immanuel Kant. Kantian ethics look to universal rules and norms, where what is considered right and good in one situation is decreed to apply more generally. Such ideas are deeply embedded in Western ways of thinking. They invoke considerations of fairness and consistency – a 'rules are rules' type of approach – whereby everyone is treated the same, often out of a fear that to treat them differently would lead to chaos or be 'unfair'. However, we have already seen that children are different (Maier, 1979) and that they need to be responded to differently. In that case, to treat young people all the same in the interests of fairness is ill conceived.

Beyond rules and rights

Legalistic and procedural ways of thinking about the complex dynamics involved in caring relationships are increasingly questioned (Meagher and Parton, 2004; Smith and Smith, 2008). Writers about care work are beginning to look beyond Kant towards alternative ethical paradigms. One alternative ethical tradition is based around the notion of virtue ethics, which reaches back to the Greek philosopher Aristotle. Virtue ethics are conceived around the moral character of the individual actor, rather than abstract rules. An Aristotelian approach applied to child care would suggest that helping children and young people develop good behaviours is about encouraging the patient acquisition of virtuous habits. This takes time and involves delaying gratification. Although children can tend to be focused on the immediate gains and benefits from a situation, they can be encouraged to develop a right sense of priorities through helping them to consider and value what may be in the future (Jones, 2010).

Good or virtuous behaviours are learned over time through exposure to, encouragement towards and the practice of particular behaviours, so that such patterns become incorporated into character traits and inform all aspects of an individual's behaviour over time. The German term for what is involved in this is *bildung* (as discussed in Chapter One); the French is *formation,* which translates directly into English. However, the concept of human formation is rarely apparent in the English-speaking world, except in religious circles. Nevertheless, it perhaps encapsulates what is involved in bringing up children and building their characters. Building character is part and parcel of upbringing.

Another ethical approach that is receiving much attention in social work and that influences our thinking in this book is that of care ethics, which foregrounds the idea that virtuous behaviours stem from the relationships that exist and develop among and between individuals. Noddings (2002a) proposes a relationally based ethic of care, which challenges theories of moral philosophy focused on rights and justice. She emphasises, instead, notions of human interconnectedness, responsibility and caring for others. As the title of one of her books suggests, Noddings (2002a) argues that the development of such qualities 'starts at home', in early family relationships. It is through the experience of care that we learn to care for one another and, indeed, to take that care and concern for the other beyond our immediate relationships to encompass wider habits of respect and responsibility, and ultimately a sense of good citizenship and social justice. From such a perspective, citizenship is not something that can be learned from school curricula but has to emerge over time through the experience and practice of caring relationships.

Noddings argues that moral development is essentially a social process that involves 'modelling, dialogue, practice and confirmation' (2002b: 148), lending itself very readily to lifespace-based models of practice. There is some resonance with social learning theories (Bandura, 1977), which call upon role models to teach a young person how to behave in pro-social ways, primarily through leading by example and reinforcing particular standards of behaviour on a day-to-day basis. Personal attributes of honesty, concern and commitment on the part of the worker and a clear definition of roles are central to the efficacy of this model (Trotter, 1999), while Brendtro and du Toit (2005) specifically identify the importance of qualities of empathy and fairness in caring adults. Children need to be surrounded by role models whom they sense to be fair and who can provide them with the kind of ethical feedback that is vital to character development. 'Feedback involves not just saying that something is wrong but working through with the child why it is wrong, in what sense it is wrong, and helping to develop strategies of understanding and insight that will enable the child to avoid acting in similar ways in the future' (Jones, 2010: 24).

Insights from the literature on virtue and care ethics would seem to resonate with a child and youth care approach to practice. Thinking back to Maier's 'core of care' (see Chapter Two), it is clear that personalised behaviour training can only be effective if it is founded upon predictable and dependable personal relationships. The development of such relationships and the resultant opportunities to influence behaviour happen in the lifespace. But, of course, many children in care have lacked this early relational care, or have experienced it as interrupted or inconsistent because of inadequate attachments or adverse experiences. The early experiences through which character is formed have not been learned, thus requiring that this process starts further down the line when children are older and patterns of behaviour more established. They need what Kilbrandon (1964), in his seminal report on juvenile delinquency, identified as additional measures of education and upbringing. Social education of this type can be conflictual and can require adults to assert a level of authority or even coercion. Kleipoedszus (2011) offers a welcome argument for relationships being forged through conflict. Children need adults who will not avoid conflict due to fear, but who will work creatively with it. There are times '– in family, school or community life – when coercion is necessary. The coercion must be for the sake of the one coerced, and it should be followed by negotiation' (Noddings, 2002a: 202). The connection created through genuine engagement and negotiation rather than artificial sensitivity makes it possible in the longer term for residential child care workers to encourage and nurture change, rather than demanding it.

Developing a respectful culture

Ensuring respectful and responsible behaviour in residential child care requires a social climate in which there is a baseline of order and organisation (Moos, 1976). Or perhaps more appropriately, to reiterate some of the messages from Chapter Two, residential child care workers need to create and sustain a social climate in which children and adults can experience a sense of safety and security, where their more troubled feelings and behaviours can be 'held' or 'contained'. When children or young people feel appropriately held or contained they can better manage experiences and emotions, thus enabling them to interact more adaptively with those around them. At one level this containment comes through basic care and the setting of boundaries. But while some controls may need to be external, order is not likely to be derived through the administration of house rules alone. As identified in Chapter Two, setting boundaries is best established through the idea of rhythm rather than rules – through the development of an overall atmosphere that absorbs or contains disturbances while also conveying acceptance, respect and understanding (Steckley, 2010). Ultimately, in such environments children can begin to work through and make sense of their feelings and experiences, and to develop their capacity to manage these in more pro-social ways.

Children are held in key relationships with their carers. Through relational connections, a young person is treated with greater respect and learns to respect, thereby laying the foundations for more responsible behaviour in the longer term. Together young people and adults 'can cultivate insight that will allow the child to develop into a person who can flourish in society and help society flourish' (Jones, 2010: 25). Getting the rhythms of daily living right can create an atmosphere where young people feel accepted, respected and understood. There are, however, a number of external factors that challenge the creation of healthy cultures of care. Specifically, admissions policies that put the most difficult to place children together in one home can result in the creation of cultures that escalate well beyond the capacities of even the best residential workers to manage effectively. Such situations frequently lead to an (understandable) over-reliance on external and sometimes physical controls.

Managing conflict

The emotion, intimacy, messiness and ambiguity that are part and parcel of residential child care all too often result in practices that are less than ideal or left open to misinterpretation; perhaps even grievances. Procedural ways of addressing such situations would seek recourse to bullying procedures if the problem were between two children. Alternatively, if such situations involve adults, the results might lead to complaints mechanisms, perhaps even leading to child protection and legal procedures. In all but the most extreme cases, such recourse may actually get in the way of proper resolution of problems between individuals. The reality is that there will be conflicts in living together, and these need to be worked through. Legalistic responses avoid such 'working through' and preclude the learning that can result from it. Cross puts this case nicely when she says that:

… children living with adults who display love and care and think in terms of putting things right, and resolving conflicts, rather than finding someone to blame, will absorb these values and act accordingly. They learn that putting things right can be a pleasant experience and can make you feel better about yourself and others.

Children are capable of understanding that different individuals who transgress the boundaries of appropriate behaviour will need different responses to help them manage better. Children are able to empathise with adults and accept that they make mistakes and may be victims of overwhelming emotions; this can happen even in situations where they have been hurt by the adult concerned.

Adults who can admit that they make mistakes don't always have the 'right' answer and can be unduly influenced by their emotions at times of stress, will – contrary to popular opinion – gain the respect of children. This does not of course mean that adults should not try to always manage their emotions in such a way that they minimise harm and distress to others. But it recognises the fact that they will not always succeed. In a culture of blame, adults will rationalise their feelings and justify their actions. Children will feel unfairly treated and will not learn that adults also have upsetting emotions that have to be managed, and when occasionally they are not, then things can go wrong; but subsequently things can be put right and reparation made. Adults are important role models for the children in this respect.

Present day emphasis on recording events and accountability in the name of child protection may prevent the spontaneous and constructive resolution of difficulties between individuals. (Cross, 2008)

Physical restraint

At the extreme end of the spectrum, containment may, on occasion, require the use of physical restraint. In recent years, the use of restraint has become a political hot potato, often considered within rights discourses and subject to myriad proprietary programmes of intervention (Smith, 2009). It is not our intention in this chapter to provide guidance on the uses of physical restraint. Such guidance applied to residential child care is available elsewhere (Davidson et al, 2005). Steckley (2010; 2011) also provides an excellent discussion on the complexities and dynamics of physical restraint. Restraint may be experienced as being abusive or, conversely, as encouraging feelings of safety and of being cared for. What is increasingly apparent is that the relationship that exists and develops between the adults and young people who are party to the exchange is central to how any use of restraint is experienced. Exercised properly, physical restraint can provide formative experiences in developing relationships of mutual trust and respect, as the following quotation suggests:

'Yes. I didn't like Mr Brown that much until he restrained me.'

Interviewer: 'Is there a trust factor involved in all that too?'

'Yes, if somebody restrains you and you trust them again, you are alright but if somebody restrains you and you don't like them you are not going to trust them but if they restrain you and they do it alright you trust them again, like me and Mr Brown, we're alright.' (Steckley and Kendrick, 2005: 19)

But while this may be so, the use of restraint should not be seen as a therapeutic intervention in itself, nor justified on such grounds alone. Restraint is sometimes necessary in pursuit of the overall aims of making children feel safe, developing respectful relationships and ensuring a holding environment that offers emotional containment. As relationships strengthen, the need for restraint can (although it will not necessarily) lessen and other less intrusive interventions such as a firm word, a request or even a subtle but deliberate raised eyebrow can help a young person manage their own behaviour (Steckley, 2005).

If the best behavioural management is undertaken in the context of relationships, the way that carers use themselves in such relationships takes on central importance. Once again, assuming that acting-out behaviour is symptomatic of some underlying need (even if it is simply a perceived need to show off to peers rather than something more deeply rooted), then to try and work out what these needs are and to intervene at an early point to attend to some of these needs, or perhaps divert attention towards alternative ways of meeting such needs, becomes the hallmark of a good residential child care worker. Garfat (1998) argues that effective interventions are those that 'fit' – those where the worker is able to intuitively work out what is going on for a particular child, to enter into a rhythm with them and to tailor an appropriate response. Thus, some young people might respond to a firm word, while others might require some gentle coaxing or explanation. Whatever technique is employed, the aim is to convey messages about what is acceptable behaviour in the expectation that this – over time – becomes internalised.

A contemporary interest in notions of restorative justice (accepting that the emphasis in many incarnations of such an approach involve a legalistic conception of justice rather than restoration) might similarly point to different ways of resolving everyday conflicts. Brendtro and du Toit (2005) highlight the competing demands of justice versus restorative models. A justice model, they say, asserts that those who hurt others must be made to suffer, whereas a restorative model claims that those who hurt others must restore broken bonds. Legalistic approaches may actually impede the mending of broken relational bonds.

Encouraging respect

Before children can demonstrate respect for others and for their environments they need to learn to respect themselves. This can only happen over time and through the experience of interactions and relationships with those around them that convey respect. Self-respect can be encouraged in daily living through adult expectations that children clean their teeth, shower or bathe regularly and wear properly laundered and appropriate clothing. Children need to feel comfortable in and with their own bodies if they are to treat these with respect and avoid the sort of situations that so many looked after young people get into, where they don't really care what happens to them, potentially leading to excessive risk-taking behaviours. Priority, too, should be given to addressing health issues – such as bad teeth, acne or being overweight – which can seriously affect children's perceptions of self-worth and identity. Involvement in sporting or other physical activities can be beneficial in helping children develop a good sense of and respect for their bodies, which in turn helps them feel more positive about themselves. As children or young people start feeling good about themselves, so it is that they frequently start treating others with greater respect.

Creating frameworks for respectful relations among and between children and staff is the starting point for ensuring respect in everyday encounters. There should be clear expectations about how people talk to one another and about what kind of language is and is not acceptable. Role-modelling and expecting the use of 'please' and 'thank you' and of asking to leave the table at the end of a meal are not simply middle-class affectations; they are fundamental to cultures of mutual respect. Swearing, even accepting that it may come as second nature for many looked after children and young people, should not be considered acceptable in settings which aim to encourage and equip young people to operate respectfully and responsibly in a range of social settings beyond the doors of residential care. Cultural relativism or arguments promoting sub-cultural norms are not particularly helpful in this respect. In social environments where the prevailing culture deems such behaviours to be unacceptable, even young people who are habitual swearers quickly learn to check their use of bad language and to apologise when a swear word slips out. In a similar vein – even when they are upset – children should be channelled towards expressing their feelings in ways that are less likely to be misunderstood in wider social contexts, and helped to develop more adaptive strategies for managing personal distress in their lives.

Respect is reciprocal; respectful relations require that all parties feel respected in order to show respect in return. Adults who allow children to swear at or otherwise abuse them do not do themselves or the children with whom they work with any favours. In such situations, young people are given a message that such adults lack self-respect. Adults who seek to nurture without setting behavioural expectations for children 'seldom have strong influence. Youth may see them as weak and they become "friends without influence"' (Brendtro and du Toit, 2005: 89). Carers have to strike an appropriate balance between nurture and high expectations, demanding responsibility rather than compliance and fostering a sense of self-efficacy, whereby children and young people can begin to take some responsibility for and control over their lives (Brendtro and du Toit, 2005). To feel confident in themselves and clear that they will not accept disrespectful behaviours, adults need to feel supported by their organisations when challenging such behaviours. This sense of confidence can be eroded very easily in practice cultures where young people are only too aware that ultimate authority lies with external managers outside the residence (Emond, 2004).

Residential child care workers can gain respect through their demeanours as well as through messages conveyed by their actions as they go about their work. Actions speak louder than words, especially in residential child care work. Looking the part and dressing to suit the occasion can promote a sense of respect, as can simple things like ensuring that daily tasks are undertaken in a timely fashion. It is important that carers are prepared for the various events and transitions of the day, from ensuring that breakfast tables are set and school clothes laid out and ready, to a readiness to greet children as they return from school. Respect emerges from the sense of dependability, reliability and authority that carers demonstrate in their everyday practice. This doesn't just happen. It emerges over time, with carers gradually progressing through an early reliance on rules and external boundaries to a place where their authority and respect derives more from the kind of relationships they are able to develop (Garfat, 2001).

Encouraging responsibility

Children and young people in care are often characterised as being irresponsible. Such an assumption can be used, in turn, to deny them responsibility, especially in risk-averse climates where carers may fear the consequences of children failing to manage any responsibility given to them.

Yet the reality is that young people only learn to become responsible if they are given responsibility. The development of responsibility in residential child care begins with responsibility in daily living. Children should be expected to take responsibility for their own living space, being required to make their bed and to keep their bedroom reasonably tidy, if need be with adult support and encouragement. Such a requirement should extend to them taking some responsibility for wider community living through expectations around undertaking chores such as setting and clearing tables, sweeping or vacuuming floors and cleaning bathrooms. The reality is that most residential child care centres will have a cleaner to do such tasks more thoroughly, but this should not be at the expense of children being given the message that they have a responsibility to themselves and other people to help maintain their immediate living environment.

Expecting that young people will take responsibility can imbue a sense of ownership and pride, thereby reinforcing a sense of belonging. In addition to everyday tasks, children can also be given particular responsibilities. For example, children can help make sure that plants are watered, fish are fed, sports equipment is maintained, tables are set or supper is prepared. Older or more established children might be asked to look out for younger or less confident residents.

A powerful way of imparting a sense of responsibility and trust is when staff can involve young people in helping them with aspects of their own lives, such as getting their help with gardening or tasks such as stripping walls. Such practices, which used to be commonplace, have unfortunately fallen prey to misconceived health and safety or safe caring agendas, or to some ill-considered notion that involvement in such tasks was exploitative and tantamount to using cheap labour. This misunderstands the nature of such practices. The reality is that children in family situations take some pride in helping with what they might perceive to be 'real work', especially if undertaken alongside adults whom they like and respect. Giving children a sense of being trusted to the extent that they can be invited into a family home and asked to help conveys a powerful message of acceptance. Carers who have engaged in such practices will know that their trust is invariably well placed in these situations. Being trusted and being able to respond with trust in controlled situations such as these often provides a platform for the development of trust and responsibility in other areas of life. The alternative is one involving low-trust relationships, where barriers and mutual suspicion between adults and children are never far from the surface.

If children are to become responsible for their actions, then this is more likely to happen when they encounter the natural consequences of things going wrong rather than when adults impose 'consequences' – which in many cases have become synonymous with punishments or sanctions. Sometimes young people need to be allowed to make mistakes and then be encouraged to work out how they might do things a bit better next time round. In a risk-averse culture, however, 'messing up' is viewed as a sign of culpability on the part of the child or the adults responsible for them instead of an opportunity for learning. The cult of the risk assessment can easily get in the way of children and young people learning responsibility.

Summary

We should not expect or accept that disrespectful or irresponsible behaviour is an inevitable feature of children in care. That said, working towards socially acceptable behaviour from young people takes persistence and the courage to address unacceptable behaviour consistently, sensitively but authoritatively. Focusing 'in a positive way on character development will create children who mature into adults who are able to play a full role in society, thereby enriching society through their contribution' (Jones, 2010: 27). Homes and schools that encourage and allow children to become 'respect-able' and 'response-able' need to include the following features:

- an environment that is safe both physically and emotionally safe; carers who are empathic and emotionally available;
- key relationships with carers in which children can feel emotionally 'held' and which can help them make sense of their experiences and feelings;
- clear and predictable boundaries, routines and structures that are applied in a child-centred and flexible way;
- a degree of tolerance related to their expression of feelings, and responses to misbehaviour that are predictable, developmentally appropriate, manageable and not punitive;
- carers who are supported by their organisation and have their needs met associated with their work of therapeutic containment.

Returning to the scenario

Often in residential child care, situations flare up and staff have to respond in the moment to manage extreme emotions and potential risk to others. We quoted the North American proverb earlier in this chapter about hurt people hurting people. Very often, personal hurt is projected onto significant figures in the lives of those we would seek to hurt – often mothers. It also surfaces oftentimes in sexual taunting. Both the targeting of significant relationships and of alleged sexual proclivities may reflect underlying anxieties around the security of these aspects of an individual's own life.

Whatever the triggers of particular flare-ups, sometimes quick and decisive action is required. Such situations provoke anxiety in staff who, through their concern that a situation does not get out of control, can compound it. In this case Scott and Liz acting with good intent ended up restraining Jane, who might be thought to be the victim of bullying but could not manage to communicate the hurt that she claims Mark had been causing her.

Difficult situations can best be brought under control where staff have a 'presence' that can communicate security and safety to children and young people. 'Presence' is hard to define but easy to notice and experience. Workers who have developed their sense of personal authority and respect create a sense of calm and security that those around them experience, often without any verbal interaction. Less experienced and insecure staff may, however, project their own anxiety into situations and unwittingly fuel the emotional climate. Developing a sense of personal authority takes time and cannot be learned from courses and training alone. Working alongside experienced workers and having access to good quality, challenging supervision, combined with open feedback from peers, can combine to help newer workers feel confident and secure in their practice.

Situations like this are rarely amenable to any formulaic anti-bullying strategies or policies. They demand that Mark be spoken to about his taunting and ideally that he can be brought round to a place where he acknowledges the unacceptability of his behaviour and can, ideally, bring himself to apologise to Jane. He, of course, will no doubt have his own side of the story to tell and this also needs to be heard. Once the initial heat has died down there may be benefit in bringing Mark and Jane together to talk through what went wrong. It is through such restorative practices, enacted within the context of fractured relationships, that healing and growth can come about.

At another level, staff members who are called to intervene in such situations can be left with a range of feelings. Scott has been faced with allegations of sexual abuse, which, on the face of it, he can interpret as an expression of Jane's hurt and distress. Such allegations can be worrying, nevertheless – especially in a climate that is inclined to overreact to any hint of abuse (Sikes and Piper, 2010) – and should be talked through with colleagues or managers and recorded in any write-up of the incident. The staff members in this situation are also left with gnawing feelings that they may have intervened too quickly and that they perhaps hadn't understood all of what was going on in the situation. They need to become comfortable working in such uncertainty, but also to reflect on it for possible future learning.

Thoughts for practice

Staff teams should discuss and set high behavioural expectations, especially around how people, young people and adults talk to one another. More importantly, they need to model these expectations in daily encounters. This will involve showing disapproval or disappointment when expectations are not met and letting children know that this is or isn't the way that things are done around here.

Think about how you might establish rhythms of care that help children or young people feel safe and respected.

Consider what might be needed to build close but suitably authoritative relationships with children and young people so that they might feel safe and 'held'. This comes from qualities of adult confidence and fairness rather than through carping or nagging.

Like most things in residential child care, respect and responsibility are encouraged in the small things. Be respectful of young people and colleagues, and expect to be respected in return. Say 'please' and 'thank you', and expect that others do so as well.

Say 'sorry' and mean it when you get things wrong. This can be one of the most powerful interventions with young people. In the same vein, model forgiveness and the acceptance of mistakes, while maintaining a desire to do better next time.

Acknowledge when children or young people act responsibly and with respect.

Set household chores and tasks, and do these alongside children or young people. Give children responsibilities, accepting that they might get things wrong. This might extend to sharing some responsibility for one another.

Arrange experiences that allow children and young people to feel good about themselves, thereby fostering a sense of self-respect.

Dress appropriately to the occasion and encourage children and young people to do likewise.

Further reading

The Native American Circle of Courage material is helpful in thinking about how children learn responsibility:

Brendtro, L., Brokenleg, M. and Van Bockern, S. (2002) *Reclaiming youth at risk: our hope for the future*, Bloomington, IN: Solution Tree;

Brendtro, L. and du Toit, L. (2005) *Response ability pathways: restoring bonds of respect*, Cape Town: PreText Publishers.

June Jones takes a welcome and much neglected look at character formation:

Jones, J. (2010) 'Raising children: a character-based approach to residential child care', *Scottish Journal of Residential Child Care*, vol 9, no 2, pp 22–7.

And Nel Noddings' work is pertinent, once again:

Noddings, N. (2002b) *Educating moral people: a caring alternative to moral education*, New York: Teachers' College Press.

8

Contributing: developing generosity

Scenario

Jason is a 14-year-old black African and has been living in a children's home on the edge of a large city for four months. He previously lived with his mother, Carole, and his three younger sisters, but had become increasingly difficult for his mother to control and was getting involved in incidents of petty crime and vandalism in his local community. He was also verbally abusive to his mother and physically hurt her on a number of occasions. Following several short-term suspensions from school for fighting and being defiant to his teachers, he was eventually excluded permanently. Jason's father, David, left the family home two years previously and has had no contact with the family since. The local authority concluded that Jason was beyond his mother's control and she agreed to his placement in the children's home.

When initially accommodated, Jason was very defiant. He has now settled really well, however, and is accepting of the structures and routines of the home. He has built good relationships with other children and staff and is described as friendly and funny. He is good at sports and has started to build up attendance at a local school. He has struck up a particularly strong relationship with his keyworker, Angela, who for her part has gone out of her way to do things with Jason, sometimes staying back after her shift has ended to do so.

Jason's relationship with his mother, however, has remained difficult. He has expressed a lot of anger about the several male partners she has had since his father left. His mother is convinced that Jason is like his father, who she describes as abusive and good for nothing. She has said that she thinks Jason is being spoiled in the children's home and that he is conning the staff with the apparent change in his behaviour. Despite these difficulties, Carole has visited Jason on a weekly basis and wants things to be better between them. Jason has said he would like to live at home again if his mother did not embarrass him by going out with different men, none of whom he likes.

Each year the children's home supports the local community gala day, and this year is helping to run a soft drinks and confectionery stall at the 10K road race, which attracts serious competitive runners but is also a fun run for all ages from the community. Funds raised are to be split between a project with which a local church group is involved to help build a school in Africa and support for the various groups running at the local community centre. Angela has asked Jason to help run the children's home stall and, as it is on the day that Jason's mum, Carole, visits, Angela also tells Jason that she has asked Carole if she would also like to come along.

Jason is initially reluctant: "What would I want to do that for?"

Angela: "It's for good causes, Jason."

Jason: "A school in Africa! What's that got to do with me?"

Angela: "It's not just the school in Africa. Some of the money will also be used to help keep the group for the older people going. That's really important for some of them, as it's maybe the only time in the week that they get out. Oh, and some of the money is also to be used to help get a new set of strips for the football team that you want to join."

Jason eventually agrees to man the stall, although both he and his mum do so with some apprehension. Jason's mum has said she does not trust Jason handling money and, with a bit of humour, she has said he will eat and drink all the stock. Jason has said he is worried that his mum will embarrass him, particularly as some of his new school friends will be around.

Angela, Jason, Carole and one of the local church group members all work for four hours on the very busy stall. Both Carole and Jason are engaging, friendly and sociable with customers and Jason has a laugh with some of his new schoolmates. Carole admits to Angela at the end of the day that she has seen Jason in a new light and likes his humour and his confidence. Jason acknowledges that working alongside his mother has been OK and she has not nagged him.

After things have been cleared away, Jason says to Angela: "That was a good laugh. What did you say the money was to be used for again?"

Angela reiterates the story about the old people's group.

Jason: "That's good. I used to help out at an old people's home when I was in the Scouts. I used to like chatting to the old people. … And that guy who is helping build the school in Africa – he was alright. He was telling me about the class sizes and how the kids there had hardly any books or things. It's sort of worthwhile what they're doing to help …"

Introduction

Contributing is about undertaking positive, caring actions that benefit others and about doing one's part to help things turn out well. A contributing young person cares about others and their wellbeing. She or he is affected by the feelings and experiences of others. This requires an ability to understand and know about others, their feelings, their culture and the things that they value or believe. Making a positive contribution is not just about doing things for others. It also involves considering how *all* of one's actions might affect other people. There are times when making a positive contribution might involve not doing something that one is tempted to do. For example, when a young person is angry and may want to strike out at someone verbally or even physically, he or she can sometimes make a positive contribution by choosing to calm her or himself, not strike out and engage in positive problem solving, thus contributing to the wellbeing of both self and other. When young people contribute to others' wellbeing they demonstrate generosity, or giving of self for the benefit of others. Generosity has been argued to be a fundamental characteristic of healthy individuals (Brendtro and du Toit, 2005).

This chapter explores the theme of generosity and some of the concepts that run alongside it. Generosity grows out of the common things of life, through everyday encounters and daily kindnesses. In helping others, young people develop their own sense of worthiness through making positive contributions to another human life. Generosity is central to one's capacity to care and to be cared for. It needs to be cultivated, however, and when it is, a sense of worth for self and others will ultimately steer young people away from anti-social behaviour, towards pro-social patterns of behaviour. We learn how to contribute to society, not so much through what we are told, but through how we are treated.

The benefits associated with children, and indeed adults, developing and practising a spirit of generosity is lent support by a number of disciplinary perspectives: philosophy, psychology and increasingly neuroscience.

We start with philosophy. According to Bauman (2000), when the biblical figure Cain asked God, "Am I my brother's keeper?" he introduced the roots of immorality to the human condition. It ought to have been evident to Cain that he was his brother's keeper, and his sister's and his neighbour's. To question this sense of obligation introduced a dissonance to the pull we feel as human beings to reach out to the other. The ancient Greeks identified different types of love, one of which – *agape* – encompassed a selfless giving, epitomised perhaps in the tale of the Good Samaritan, who reached out to the stranger in a situation where it might have been easier not to. It is an aspect of our humanity that we are drawn to do so.

Tronto (1994) notes that much contemporary ethical thinking is rooted in the philosophers of the Scottish Enlightenment. Francis Hutcheson (1694–1746), for example, then Professor of Moral Philosophy at the University of Glasgow, argued that humans are imbued with natural feelings of benevolence. Such feelings guide their moral acts and instil an innate moral sense which informs their moral judgements, leading them to reach out to the other(s) with generosity.

This strand of thinking lost out to a dominant Enlightenment belief that reason rather than emotion should define and guide human actions, and that these should be separated out from one another. Qualities of reason and dispassion were thus given prominence (Tronto, 1994) and became particularly influential in social work as it developed as a profession. The pre-eminent position given to such qualities has led to understandings of caring relations founded upon notions of duty and contractual obligation, dissipating a primary impulse to care. Reaching out to the other, according to dominant ideas of what it means to be 'professional' can thus be construed as 'unprofessional'.

Altruism, empathy and sympathy

A general predisposition towards concern for the wellbeing of others and for doing good might be termed altruism. A growing body of research suggests that powerful benefits are evident in the mental and physical wellbeing of the altruistic individual (Brendtro and du Toit, 2005). Altruism on its own, however, can be an abstraction. We can be altruistic when, for instance, we give money to charity, but this does not involve us in direct engagement with the object of our charity. The quality of empathy (called sympathy in some of the literature) takes altruism into the realm of personal feelings for a concrete individual, allowing us to take the perspective of another. Compassion takes empathy or sympathy to the next level, in that it includes the need or desire to take the next step and to do something to alleviate suffering.

The psychologist Martin Hoffman describes empathy as 'the spark of human concern for others, the glue that makes social life possible' (2000: 3). Hoffman views empathy as a biologically based disposition for altruistic behaviour, which allows us to respond to a variety of cues from another person – a tendency that is apparent from infancy. Children appreciate the opportunity to care for others, to contribute and to be experienced as helpful.

Philosophical and psychological perspectives on empathy are increasingly supported by developments in neuroscience. We are, it seems, hard wired for empathy (Iacoboni, 2008). The mirror neurons in our brains are activated by others' actions, expressions and emotions and act to imitate these as though the observers were sharing the same experience themselves. Any neuroscientific predisposition towards the other is, not surprisingly, mediated by social conditions and experiences. The empathic development of many children in care can be disrupted or distorted by previous experience. They may have had to take care of themselves as others have not taken care of them in the way they should have. Consequently, such children may mistrust adults and adult expressions of generosity (Smart, 2010). They may come across as selfish, grasping and closed. They may respond to previous experiences by resisting or exploiting kindness. They may seek to provoke the unkindness or rejection that characterised previous relationships. At another level, they may be burdened by guilt, imagining themselves responsible for things that have gone wrong in their families. These ways of 'being in the world', while not necessarily adaptive, may have kept children safe, helped them feel in control and given their life meaning and structure.

Empathy can be reinforced through the experience and practice of nurturing and interdependent relationships (Perry and Szalavitz, 2010). Mirror neurone activity is stimulated in children who grow up in a stable and nurturing emotional environment, and through this they develop and learn to demonstrate empathic responses. Children, on the other hand, who have experienced neglect or a lack of continuity of care experience less brain activity of this kind. This should not be taken to imply any permanent impairment. One of the problems with neuroscientific perspectives applied to social settings is that they can be interpreted too deterministically. The brain, in fact, demonstrates a remarkable plasticity and continues to develop and adapt throughout life. So children and young people can, in conducive environments, learn how to respond better to others. One of the tasks of residential child care, therefore, is to 'massage the numb values' (Redl, 1966) that lie dormant in children and young people.

A sense of empathy can lead to feelings of guilt or pangs of conscience when we fail to respond empathically. While carers should try to avoid making children feel guilty, they should nevertheless be concerned about the development of conscience. Parents and carers, within the context of caring relationships and not in a nagging or sanctimonious way, need to point out the effects of a child or young person's behaviour on other people and how their behaviour makes others feel. This is vital to the development of pro-social behaviours.

Autism

Some children — boys in particular — who function within the autistic spectrum may find it difficult to discern or respond to kindness because of the way that their brains are configured (Baron-Cohen, 2008). Baron-Cohen's research identifies autism as a condition that occurs at the extreme end of an empathy continuum. The kind of struggles autistic children experience in social situations are a consequence of their difficulties in picking up social cues from those around them; basically, a difficulty in empathising. It may be helpful to think in terms of empathy existing or happening on a continuum, with some being better at empathising than others.

Kindness – going the extra mile

When we act on feelings of compassion this behaviour becomes an act of kindness (Long, 2007). To experience kindness as helpful, rather than to regard it with suspicion, depends in turn on a sense of trust. Trust is described as an emotional bond between people that cannot be won or awarded. It is based on a relationship that must be earned slowly over time. To trust someone is to believe that they will not exploit or betray your confidence. It involves an element of dependability. In this sense it has resonances with Maier's conceptualisation of the 'core of care' discussed in Chapter Two, whereby elements of predictability and dependability develop out of the relationship building process. Trust, therefore, is built up and requires commitment over time.

Things that get in the way of generosity

Threats to generosity are all too apparent within neoliberal political and economic systems, which stress the primacy of the individual and of individual rights and responsibilities. Notions of care and vocation, and of reaching out to others, can be viewed as quaint or even suspicious. Care is reduced to a bottom-line economic calculation, increasingly subject to market forces and to crude managerial means of control. According to Brannen and Moss:

> 'new capitalism' calls for individualism, instrumental rationality, flexibility, short-term engagement, de-regulation and the dissolution of established relationships and practices, caring relationships ... are predicated on an expressive rather than instrumental relationship to others (based on) trust, commitment over time and a degree of predictability. (2003: 202)

Practice can be driven by an ill-conceived pursuit of 'what works' or 'evidence-based' programmes that promise to deliver more measurable and efficient outcomes of interventions. To a large extent, this is a false promise.

'What works' isn't working: despite all the gloss, talk of improvement and modernisation, care has not necessarily become a better place for children. It has lost much of its sense of moral and professional purpose (Webb, 2010).

Academics (for example, Meagher and Parton, 2004; Smith and Smith, 2008; White, 2008) increasingly question the way that notions of care and relationship are reduced to economic and administrative categories within contemporary social work and social care. These writers argue the need to reclaim a wider moral or ethical purpose for caring – a sense of purpose that moves beyond rules and regulations and back to that innate desire to reach out to others with generosity of spirit; something that is not rational or measurable. Bauman goes so far as to argue that 'Morality is endemically and irredeemably non-rational – in the sense of not being calculable, hence not being presentable as following impersonal rules' (1993: 60). He further claims:

> There is nothing reasonable about taking responsibility, about caring and being moral. Morality has only itself to support it: it is better to care than to wash one's hands, better to be in solidarity with the unhappiness of the other than indifferent. (Bauman 2000: 11)

But caring is not as simple as merely responding to a moral impulse to reach out to the other in their time of need. To encounter another person's distress can be emotionally difficult, so much so that we can seek to remove or at least minimise the emotional content of caring relationships. It is interesting to note how, more than 60 years ago, Menzies Lyth (1960) identified a similar organisational dynamic in her seminal work 'A case-study in the functioning of social systems as a defence against anxiety', a study of ward nurses caring for acutely ill patients. Menzies Lyth identified a number of strategies that nurses brought to bear in protecting themselves from the strong feelings evoked by their patients, all of which operated to place a distance between them and the objects of their care. This can be rationalised in some of the professional literature as a necessary 'professional distance'.

'Distance' is a problem in relational work but is increasingly expected within bureaucratic systems. Bauman (1993) argues that social distance, which does not involve direct face-to-face contact with another person, is *in extremis* linked with de-humanising practices, as people make decisions and engage in actions that do not take into account the impact of these decisions on concrete human beings and situations. Social distance is evident in residential child care practice, which falls back on rules and procedures, and in which superficiality is a common dynamic affecting the depth and meaning attached to adult–child relationships. Carers can come over as cold and awkward, both practically and emotionally. They can be cast as detached providers of a clinical and sanitised care, bereft of feelings (Ricks, 1992).

A care ethics approach to generosity

Feminist philosophers have argued that altruistic dispositions such as caring, compassion, and love should be made the focus of morality. These philosophers claim that relationships rather than rules should be at the heart of morality and that most of our relationships are not only intimate but also involuntary. In many respects we cannot avoid the strong feelings that draw us towards many of the children with whom we work, yet we are forced within current ways of thinking to consider these to be unprofessional. Such a view of professionalism gets in the way of care through denying the authentic friendships that need to be at the centre of caring relations.

Increasingly, the user and carer movement in social work challenges us to reconsider what kind of relationships children in residential care might want from an adult. McLeod (2010) identifies the importance of children in care feeling that their wellbeing is promoted through having a positive and sustained personal relationship with their social worker. A good social worker is experienced as a 'friend' and an 'equal'. In another study, a former resident remembers her carers as "fantastic people, lovely persons who are with me even now …" (Halvorsen, 2009: 72). Former clients valued adults who had time to spend on them, who spoke to, instead of at them. Halvorsen concludes that those in receipt of professional services want 'ordinary friendship where they meet on equal terms, not as client and "helper"' (2009: 76). Listening to the voices of those who have been through the care system describing what was important to them might suggest that we revisit our understandings of what it means to be professional. Debate around practices such as taking children into carers' own homes – what used to be a fairly commonplace practice – is generally nowadays proscribed but needs to be reopened. Even to suggest this can sound heretical, but our understandings of personal/professional relationships were not always what they have become. Ray Jones, a professor and former director of social work recalls that:

> As a social worker in the 1970s it was OK for me, when visiting a frail and older lady, to fill up her coal bucket and get her fire lighted. And as a team manager, three brothers living nearby, who sometimes bounced into care for short times, used to turn up at my house, and would play with my two little children. (2009)

He goes on to argue that the prominence given to systems rather than to expressions of humanity is becoming the norm all over the public sector and leads to people retreating from engaging with others. (For a good debate about the particular practice of taking children home see: www.cyc-net. org/threads/boundaries2005.html)

Generosity and gratitude in the context of paid labour

What differentiates professional care from familial care or everyday friendship is that workers are, generally, paid – although in some settings such as the Camphill schools or the L'Arche communities, both of which are based around a concept of community living this may not always be the case. Experiencing generosity from a paid carer could result in an uncomfortable sense of indebtedness. On a more positive note, acts of generosity can lead to feelings of gratitude. What seems to differentiate between whether one experiences indebtedness or gratitude is a sense that a caregiver acts out of goodwill rather than duty, and that care is provided in a respectful manner (Mullin, 2011). Unlike indebtedness, gratitude is implicated in the development of reciprocal and positive relationships between caregivers and care receivers. Such feelings transcend the fact that a carer may be paid to do so, for those experiencing respectful and relational care can discern that carers are not just motivated by money (Mullin, 2011).

Care ethics, once again, offer a useful perspective on what it is to care and be cared for, rooting care in concern and feeling for the other. Tronto (1994) identifies four elements to an ethic of care. Carers need to demonstrate attentiveness – they need to be available to the other, to convey the sense that they and perhaps only they matter at that particular moment. It's all too easy in the hustle and bustle of residential care not to pay attention to children. We can all probably recognise in colleagues and ourselves that tendency to fob children off, to tell them we'll attend to something later.

Caring also demands that carers take responsibility for caring – saying they care isn't enough: they need to act to give expression to that care. How they do so derives from implicit cultural practice rather than formal rules. Thus, when a child falls over and hurts him or herself, we know that we should comfort them in a way that is culturally appropriate. In most cultures that will involve a physical expression of concern, cleaning and dressing any wound. Formal rules and regulations which attempt to circumscribe how we should respond on such occasions actually get in the way of cultural rituals of caring. There are times when we just know how we ought to respond in particular circumstances to particular children. There are rarely any universal 'best practices' that we can call upon in such situations.

Good intentions are not sufficient in the care of others. Tronto's third element of care requires competence. There is no point in intervening in a child's life if that intervention may do more harm than good, irrespective of what our intentions might be. There needs to be an awareness of and intentionality about what carers do. The final of Tronto's four elements of an ethic of care is responsiveness. Carers are to be aware of the vulnerability of others, and respond to their needs in a way that they would want us to respond. That requires that we tailor care to the needs of the individual; as Maier (1979) says, 'it's different strokes for different blokes'. Responsiveness also calls us to be aware of how issues of power, prejudice and dependency can enter into relationships (Ward, 2006).

Within a care ethics paradigm, the one caring and the one cared for are thrown together in a relationship in which power dynamics are complex and non-linear – emotional rather than instrumental – and where there are feelings and needs on both sides. The development of a spirit of generosity and moral development evolve and unfold within the context of the relationship and are created within such relationship (Ricks and Bellefeuille, 2003).

Generosity of spirit

Generosity of spirit is a particularly appealing quality. It can lead individuals to approach situations with a sense of openness and even wonder, and to reach out to others in such a spirit. A further dimension to generosity of spirit is that of forgiveness. The act of forgiveness is well established as a universal principle among all religions. Forgiveness can be a kind and liberating way of purging acts of wrongdoing and feelings of guilt. It wipes the slate clean and gives others an opportunity to begin again without any handicapping conditions (Long, 2007).

Forgiveness presupposes an element of fallibility within the human condition. Fallibility refers to the space made for mistakes and flexibility, the ability to learn from these and adapt accordingly. Humility underlies both characteristics. In lifespace work, children's mistakes should be seen as opportunities for growth and learning. This approach is only effective, however, when the residential cultures can hold and promote a congruent perspective about the errors of staff. Practice can often be distorted by cultures of blame, making it unsafe for adults to acknowledge mistakes. Yet there is something very human about fallibility. Mistakes made in an earnest attempt at caring are not only forgivable but can provide opportunities for growth and learning (Steckley and Smith, 2011).

Other cultures' perspectives on generosity

Developing nations and indigenous cultures consider the teaching of generosity as a central aspect of bringing up children. According to Archbishop Tutu:

Africans have this thing called Ubuntu. It is about the essence of being human, it is part of the gift that Africa will give the world. It embraces hospitality, caring about others, being able to go the extra mile for the sake of others. We believe that a person is a person through another person, that my humanity is caught up, bound up, inextricably, with yours. When I dehumanise you, I inexorably dehumanise myself. The solitary human being is a contradiction in terms and therefore you seek to work for the common good because your humanity comes into its own in belonging. (Tutu, n/d)

The book *Reclaiming youth at risk* (Brendtro et al, 2002) and the wider 'Reclaiming Youth' movement draws upon Native American child-rearing practices to develop a model of how to work with troubled youth. Within Native American traditions:

virtue was reflected in the pre-eminent value of generosity. The central goal in Native American child-rearing is to teach the importance of being generous and unselfish. In the words of a Lakota Elder, 'You should be able to give away your most cherished possession without your heart beating faster'. In helping others, youth create their own proof of worthiness: they make a positive contribution to another human life. (Reclaiming Youth International, 2012)

Giving to others and giving back to the community are core values in many indigenous cultures, where adults stress generosity and unselfishness to young people as contributing to the good of all. Helping others teaches young people about connection and interdependence with other human beings. Learning that they are interrelated to each other in the community helps form a sense of obligation to other people and caring beyond one's immediate family (Lickona, in Smart, 2010).

Children who have the opportunity to give to others are more likely to develop caring qualities such as altruism, sharing, loyalty, empathy and pro-social attitudes and behaviours. Without the opportunity to experience generosity, children may appear selfish, affectionless, exploitative and to engage in anti-social behaviours. A spirit of generosity helps young people tune in and respond to the feelings of others. Helping others gives the helper a sense of self-worth and teaches them a sense of connection and interdependence (Fulcher and Garfat, 2008). Once such feelings exist then everyday relationships become more meaningful and less governed by rules and regulations. Opportunities begin to open up for further growth through the expression and practice of qualities of understanding and forgiveness, for instance.

An apology to one we have offended can also be a form of generosity, because it puts one in a position of humility. Even more powerful is the generosity of forgiveness extended to those who have hurt us. The less they deserve it, the greater the gift. Such generosity heals hurt and hatred (Brokenleg, 1999).

Staff kindness

Kindness, as we have noted, is a behaviour driven by the feeling of compassion. Compassion develops when we take seriously someone else's predicament and troubles, which may, in turn, lead to acts of kindness. In residential care, acts of kindness may emerge from the desire to respond to a child's sense of upset or distress, or indeed their happiness.

One obvious way to demonstrate kindness is through the giving and receiving of gifts. In a 'professional' climate, circumscribed by codes of conduct, such actions can be considered suspect or may even be prohibited, or at very least bound up in various protocols about recording any such instances. Such organisational expectations get in the way of spontaneity and authenticity in what are natural human interactions and exchanges. Children may give staff things they have made and these should be accepted graciously. Carers may wish to give children small birthday or Christmas presents and to do so can be very meaningful and formative in the context of their particular relationship. There is something very different about getting a present from 'the unit' and getting a gift from a liked individual. Small gestures such as buying children juice or an ice cream with one's own money, or taking them for lunch without having to go through the embarrassment of asking for receipts, achieves a symbolic importance to children and can be similarly rewarding for carers, who may want to express their feelings for a child or children in such small but personalised ways. As with any other practice, it requires the exercise of reflection and judgement as to with whom and why we might give and receive gifts, but it is at this level that such decisions should rest rather than falling back on procedure.

We have already suggested that experiencing generosity and a worker giving something of themselves in a professional relationship can have positive spin-offs. An example of this is apparent in the following quotation relating to a young offender's relationship with his probation officer and how this became implicated in the development of more pro-social behaviour:

> 'If I got in trouble now, I'd feel that I'd let Pam down – like your mum and your dad – that's the kind of relationship that it is. I'd be disappointed that I'd disappointed her. It helped too that my social worker told me personal things, so I told her things – I didn't expect

her to tell me things – but she felt relaxed enough to do this for me. It's about relationship, and trust and respect for each other. I feel like I've changed – I won't get into trouble again.' (Mark, quoted in Cree and Davis, 2007: 150)

Kindness within the resident group

It can be easy to dismiss the potential for kindness within groups of children in care. As Emond (2004) points out, discussion of the resident group is too often framed in terms of abuse and harm, where peer pressure and bullying are identified as dominant experiences. In fact, young people in care settings offer one another considerable support and kindness and demonstrate positive, caring behaviours more frequently than negative or aggressive ones (Emond, 2004). Specifically, peers are involved in offering support and advice to fellow residents and in sharing material possessions. Emond identifies the assumption, historically, that children in residential care would look after one another and discusses in her study of a Cambodian orphanage (2010) how this is still very much the case in other cultures. Frampton (2004), in his autobiography about being brought up in a Barnardo's orphanage, similarly identifies the importance of the resident group in caring for one another.

As stated at the beginning of this chapter, qualities of generosity, kindness and contributing need to be cultivated, and they need a conducive context in which to develop. White (2008) likens such an environment in which love might grow to a compost heap, requiring social compost: ideas of covenant, celebration, spirituality and healthy patterns of life – all of which provide a medium for the growth of love. A residential community might, of course, become such an environment, and it is worth consciously considering how particular elements are introduced and blended within the lifespace to help promote generosity.

Summary

We often think of generosity as something that is a one-way experience, either in terms of giving or receiving. It is, however, a more dynamic and reciprocal process than this. In giving, we also receive. A number of perspectives identify generosity or reaching out to others as an innate human instinct. For many children in care, that instinct may have been dulled as a result of past experiences, or may be well defended. Adults may also hide their moral impulses to do good or to reach out to others behind particular views of professionalism which stress objectivity and distance. Generosity can be modelled through expressions of human kindness and of adults giving of themselves in relationships with children and young people. In such relationships children value everyday 'friendship', where hierarchical and ostensibly 'professional' barriers are relaxed. Through the experience of such friendships and human connections, children and young people can themselves begin to respond with generosity.

Returning to the scenario

Jason's family difficulties have resulted in a number of relationship breakdowns and increasing involvement in anti-social behaviours. Partly because of this, and partly because he is a 14-year-old boy and being seen to be helpful is not immediately associated with being cool, Jason is initially resistant to the suggestion to become involved in the gala day. In particular, he does not see the relevance of helping a cause that seems so far removed from his own experience. Angela has to persuade him to participate, partly by explaining some of the more immediate and recognisable benefits that will accrue to the community. Essentially, she is encouraging Jason towards pro-social involvement. She is helped in so doing by being perceived by Jason as someone who has reached out to him and gone 'the extra mile' to support him. Helping on the stall has a number of benefits. On the one hand, sharing in an activity has allowed for a more relaxed and enjoyable relationship to be re-established between Jason and his mum. This might be thought of as an example of the social pedagogic concept of the common third, whereby their relationship is mediated by the activity as a third object. At another level, through participating in this event, Jason feels good about having given of his time for a good cause. Doing so then allows him to begin to make connections in his head about the recipients of his actions – in the first instance the local older people – but through this to extend his perspective to consider those further afield. In so doing he may be awakened to consider some of his own cultural heritage. His response leaves the door open to encourage him towards greater community involvement. Feeling good about his involvement in this event may also have positive and restorative spin-offs in respect of his relationship with his mother. She, for her part, might begin to reconsider her view that Jason is being 'spoiled' in the children's home when she can see that his experiencing kindness there may be paying dividends in the way he treats others.

Thoughts for practice

Children and young people will learn generosity most effectively through experiencing it from those around them. Staff should therefore consider how they might model generosity. Try and notice generosity in others and comment on it. Point out what children and colleagues do well rather than what they get wrong.

Small gestures demonstrate generosity – give children your last sweetie, buy them an ice cream; you may even use your own money at times to do so. Do things above and beyond the call of duty – this might involve doing things with children outside your work hours, such as going to watch children play school or club football – children will notice such acts of generosity

It's OK to let children know that you like them and like being with them – as individuals, as friends and as equals.

Find ways for young people to help others in everyday life – encourage them to do some voluntary work. 'Let me get that for you'; 'Can I do that for you?' – these simple yet powerful reminders contribute to the betterment of others, with kindness, on a daily basis.

You might promote the idea of giving to charity – consider organising sponsored events for particular causes.

Think about the quality of generosity of spirit and what this might mean in residential child care. Be positive and optimistic – convey the message that the world, despite the fact that many children have a raw deal in it, can be a good place.

Share stories of how you have experienced generosity in your life. We have all had such experiences and it is nice to reflect back on them – as you tell the story, the young person will experience your appreciation.

Demonstrate forgiveness when you've been wronged, and say sorry when you have got something wrong.

Take opportunities that arise to discuss important religious, political or other figures who have emphasised the importance of giving, kindness and contributing to the wellbeing of others.

For some children, pets can be a good way to develop characteristics of generosity. We can 'wonder' about how a pet sees our actions. We can give to a pet through feeding and grooming. We can give to the home by helping the pet to go for walks and stay healthy.

Further reading

Again, the Native American Circle of Courage material provides a good and accessible account of children's need for generosity:Brendtro, L., Brokenleg, M. and Van Bockern, S. (2002) *Reclaiming youth at risk: our hope for the future*, Bloomington, IN: Solution Tree; Brendtro, L. and du Toit, L. (2005) *Response ability pathways: restoring bonds of respect*. Cape Town: PreText Publishers.

Another book infused with a moral purpose to care, including discussion of generosity is:

White, K. J. (2008) *The growth of love: understanding the five essential elements of child development*, Abingdon: The Bible Reading Fellowship.

9

Included: a sense of community participation

Scenario

An inner-city children's home cares for six teenagers from different ethnic backgrounds. The composition of the staff group is predominantly white and female. Over the past few months, the home has worked to establish weekly community meetings where children and staff review all aspects of life in the house and contribute ideas about how things might be improved.

The meeting begins with refreshments of tea, coffee, juice and biscuits. An agenda is prepared in advance, based on issues that have been raised by either young people or staff. Residents can also raise issues that come up in the course of the meeting. Staff and young people rotate the chairing of meetings. Minutes are taken by one of the staff members or, occasionally, by one of the young people if they feel confident enough to do so. This adds a layer of importance and formality to the proceedings.

Some staff expressed initial misgivings about young people's capacity to chair the meetings. All of those who have participated in the meetings, however, have responded positively. Involvement in the community meeting is now highly regarded among all the residents, with noticeable improvements in self-esteem and confidence. The scope of the meeting has grown over the course of its short life. Discussions have taken place about extending its role to include the involvement of children and young people in staff recruitment, although this has not happened yet.

During a recent meeting the following dialogue ensued, initiated by 15-year-old Anwar.

Anwar: "How come there are no black guys working in this place? Or hardly any guys at all – all the boys here agree that there should be more guys working here – probably most of the girls agree as well."

Jean (the senior member of staff attending the meeting): "Well, it's not that simple. We can't just appoint black staff or guys – there are rules we have to follow to make sure the interviews are fair and that the best person in the interviews gets the job."

Anwar: "The kind of guys I think would be good to work here might not have the best qualifications. I'm not complaining, like, but there are things that white people don't get about my background. And there are times that all the boys in the home would prefer to have male staff around to do things with them or just to talk to."

Dave (14): "Yeah, Anwar is right, what about that really cool guy who came the last time. He was really good at sport and understood our music. Why didn't he get a chance?"

Jean: "I can't say exactly, but others were better in the interviews."

Dave: "Yeah, but some people can talk better than others. The thing is, we all liked him and you guys didn't."

Jean: "I do understand what you're saying, and I take the point that we need to find ways of getting you all involved and hear your opinions."

Anwar: "Yeah, how can we get our choice."

Jean: "OK. What about we spend time at the next meeting thinking about how you guys can get more involved when we next have a vacancy. Maybe you also need to understand the rules we have to follow. Perhaps we can find a way to work together on this."

Anwar, Dave and others agree this would be a good idea.

Introduction

'Inclusion' has become a central political concern in recent years. The New Labour Government elected in 1997 initiated a broad social and public policy push around the notion of social inclusion. Levitas (1998), however, identified social inclusion as proposed by New Labour as being oriented towards tackling deprivation and inequality through individual opportunity. A focus on such individualised notions of social inclusion can be argued to deflect attention away from the very apparent structural inequalities that prevent children and young people from becoming full members of society. More recent political dialogue has centred around the notion of the 'Big Society', which politicians claim is motivated by a sense of common purpose and inclusion.

A focus on inclusion, however, also presupposes an experience or experiences of exclusion. Excluding forces operate at levels of structural disadvantage but also in a lack of understanding, which can result in prejudice and fear of difference. This chapter explores how looked after children can be excluded by virtue of their socioeconomic circumstances, gender, sexual orientation and cultural identities, and how residential child care might provide opportunities for them to feel more included within their immediate communities and in society more generally. We consider developments in thinking about children's rights and ideas of participation, and also how ideas of social capital might offer a useful lens through which to consider how children might be encouraged to become full and valued members of society. A proper sense of inclusion in residential child care involves children and young people feeling understood and comfortable, whatever their backgrounds and orientations. We take the view that inclusion becomes a way of thinking within which children and their families are offered the opportunity fully to participate in events and developments (Clough and Nutbrown, 2005). How carers interact with young people in everyday encounters can facilitate a sense of inclusion and of being valued.

Sources of exclusion

Poverty and inequality

Throughout its history, residential child care has played a role in processing the children of lower income families. In their classic study, Bebbington and Miles (1989) compared the backgrounds of children admitted to care in the 1980s with a previous study from the 1960s. They found levels of deprivation in this population had actually increased over the period, identifying a litany of disadvantage: low income, poor housing and marital discord.

Of greater significance than poverty alone, however, is the level of inequality that exists in a society. This has been found to have an impact on a range of social problems: life expectancy, homicide rates, levels of violence, educational attainment and also on levels of trust and social cohesion within society (Wilkinson and Pickett, 2009). Widening inequality has been apparent across OECD countries in the past decade, with the highest levels being found in the US, Ireland and the UK (Moss and Petrie, 2002). UNICEF (2007) noted a stark divide between Northern European countries, where child wellbeing is at its highest in the Netherlands, Sweden, Denmark and Finland. The United Kingdom and the United States – countries that have embraced neoliberalism most enthusiastically – are found at the bottom of the rankings on measures of child wellbeing. This can be manifest in more fractious intergenerational relationships and in children's subjective accounts of wellbeing. Children in residential care, almost invariably, exist on the wrong end of the inequality continuum.

Professional discourses

At another level, children can also be excluded, ironically, by political and professional discourses. Since the murder of 2-year-old Jamie Bulger in Liverpool in 1993 by two 10-year-old boys, UK governments have adopted increasingly punitive and stigmatising youth justice policies. The last 20 years have seen a growth in the use of secure accommodation and secure treatments centres, as well as the introduction of a range of measures including Anti-Social Behaviour Orders, electronic tagging and curfews.

Discourses of risk and child protection can also act to exclude children in care from normal everyday experiences such as staying overnight at a friend's house or playing five-a-side football with adults who may not all be vetted by the police. Further examples of how professional ideologies can serve to exclude are evident, ironically, within discourses of normalisation and inclusion themselves. Such terms can be used to legitimate ideological preferences and, in many cases, cost-cutting measures designed to keep young people out of care. In so doing, they often misrepresent the literature on which such arguments claim to be based. Ideologies that seek to assert a moral and empirical superiority for community-based resources over residential care are often misinterpreted and misapplied.

Wolfensberger (1980), for instance, who is often cited in support of principles of normalisation, actually moved away from this term towards that of social role 'valorisation', which he saw as the enhancement of the social role of individuals or groups at risk of being socially devalued. The roles of marginalised individuals can be valued in residential as well as community settings. Paradoxically, according to Jackson, 'instead of being genuinely enabling, ideology is being deployed to support policies which place a low tolerance on diversity ... and which offer only rhetorical and not real opportunity' (2011: 3).

At another level, professional ideologies that keep children and young people in home settings when such settings leave them isolated, rather than active participants within communities, risk being excluding. On the other hand, residential child care regimes that fail to link children proactively to wider communities and opportunities, under misguided notions of normalisation, are equally likely to exclude them from meaningful community participation.

Gender

In the context of responding appropriately to difference in residential child care we now consider questions of gender. Residential child care is an obviously gendered site of practice, where around two thirds of those working in the field are women and an inverse proportion of those placed there are boys (Smith, 2010b). Ward noted back in 1993 that understandings of gender are 'virtually invisible in the group care literature' (Ward, 1993: 35). Such issues are not much better addressed today, since they are generally considered within an equal opportunities framework that fails to appreciate the often different needs of boys and girls.

In psychological terms, and accepting differences among categories, boys and girls differ collectively on just about every dimension that has been investigated (Benenson, 2005). Differences are apparent in the ways they respond, and are responded to, from a very early age. Girls generally appear more securely attached; boys respond less well to separation, especially from their mothers (Head, 1999). Boys are more likely to have problems with reading and writing, psychosocial problems and attention deficit disorders. About 70% of those in special education are boys.

Boys and girls also appear to demonstrate different patterns of seeking help (Daniel et al, 2005), with girls generally better able to ask for adult help and to use friendship networks for support. They are also differentially vulnerable to abuse and its consequences. Girls are more prey to sexually abusive behaviour and sexualised bullying, which, in light of the pre-existing vulnerability of girls in residential care, poses implications for their experiences there. The experience of sexual abuse for boys may threaten their sense of masculinity and raise fears about their sexual identity (Daniel et al, 2005). In residential care settings this can be manifest by boys 'doing gender' in compensatory hyper-masculine ways. They are more likely to be involved in serious offences such as carrying a weapon, housebreaking, robbery or theft from cars (Smith and McAra, 2004). They are also less likely to grow out of offending behaviour. Moffitt et al (2001) argue that the neuropsychological patterns that lead to lifelong persistent delinquency are much more common in boys than girls, whereas the factors underlying 'normal' offending in adolescence are the same in both sexes (Smith and McAra, 2004: 21).

Boys and girls in residential care seem to respond differentially to adult traits and dispositions. Girls appear to prefer staff who are friendly and nice, who make it safe for them to show how they feel and who are sensitive to them when they are experiencing hard times. Boys prefer staff who will talk and joke with them, who play sport and who are deemed to be fair (Nicolson and Artz, 2003). A European study looking at the difference between male and female teachers or pedagogues towards the behaviour of 'unruly' boys suggests that males can distinguish better between playing and aggression among boys than their female colleagues, who tend to view unruly play more as aggression, while males are more likely to regard it as typical boyish behaviour (Tavecchio, 2003). So, once again, we are drawn back to Maier's (1979) exhortation to be are aware of, and to respond accordingly to, the different needs and temperaments of individuals. Being careful not to fall into the trap of essentialising particular behaviours with boys and girls, and thus responding to them as categories rather than as unique individuals, residential child care needs, nevertheless, to take sex and gender into account at more sophisticated levels than within an equal opportunities framework with all that entails in terms of treating everyone the same.

Young people who are gay, lesbian or transgender are often viewed as being 'different' by other young people, and are frequently subjected to harassment and bullying (Sutherland, 2009). Residential child care workers need to work towards creating environments of safety where they, like any other young people can say, 'I feel good here.' Sexual bullying may be too easily dismissed as a simple ritual of adolescence but it may have the effect of ensuring that gay or lesbian young people 'stay in the closet' because their sexual orientation is so often met with rejection or even abuse.

Gender and sexual identities both need to be factored in to how residential child care responds to difference. The Gender Equality Duty, a legal obligation that came into force in the UK in 2007, requires that public authorities and publicly funded services promote gender equality and tackle sex discrimination. Although the implications of this legislation are not fully realised, it ought to mean that public bodies take steps to address the differential needs of boys and girls and support both mothers and fathers to parent their children. The Gender Equality Duty may establish a framework of approaches to gender that become more sensitive and sophisticated than previously brought to bear in work with children. The concept of gender pedagogy identified in some North European countries is premised on a belief that 'boys and girls and men and women behave in different ways, and all children should have the experience of both male and female ways of caring – a gender-blind approach ignores important differences' (Owen, 2003: 102).

'Race' and culture

In an increasingly multi-cultural world where residential child care needs to respond to new challenges, such as dealing with asylum-seeking children, it is important that carers respond in culturally appropriate ways. Not infrequently, it is the visual characteristic of race that is mistakenly used to distinguish between children or young people. A box on the intake form is ticked without much thought given to the meaning of generalisations such as 'South Asian', 'East European' or 'African-Caribbean', other than to acknowledge visibly distinguishing racial characteristics. Statistics that document the racial type or ethnicity of children, without reference to their culture, can serve to reinforce cultural racism. Through labelling, such practices confer institutional disadvantage around some young people more than others. If each child or young person is to *feel* included – as well as *be* included – in the daily life of those around them at home, at school, in local neighbourhoods and in their wider community, then carers need to connect with potentially marginalised young people for who they are and acknowledge what makes them special, not simply respond to a racial type.

Without reference to a cultural identity and personal systems of meaning, generalisations based on racial type offer little practical assistance and do little to support inclusion. In their encounters with residential child care workers, social workers, foster carers, teachers, police officers and other adults, minority ethnic youths may draw upon socialisation experiences and may respond in such ways that are 'often reactive to hostility and misunderstanding from the majority' (Ballard, 1979: 152–3).

Working with children and young people from diverse cultural backgrounds can be both challenging and rewarding for carers. How carers and those cared for make meaning of their first encounter, as strangers to one another, is central to the nature and strength of future relationships. Rituals of encounter between people are always grounded in cultural protocols (Leigh, 1998). In most Western societies this may be a simple handshake or, increasingly, in a digital age, the kind of conventions that attach to various social networking media. In less Westernised societies, rituals of encounter can assume deeper significance. In order to demonstrate sufficient cultural awareness workers should pay attention to questions around features of dress and public behaviour; greetings and initiation of exchanges; dialogue and interpersonal communications; the preparation and taking of food and drink; hygiene and personal space; status hierarchies and junior–senior relations; and religious, ethnic and social differences within the same cultural groups.

As noted earlier, cultural safety and security involves the state of being in which a child or young person experiences that their personal wellbeing, as well as their social and cultural frames of reference, are acknowledged – even when not fully understood by carers assigned tasks of helping them. It requires that each child or young person be provided with reasons to feel hopeful that their needs will be addressed, in terms that they understand. Cultural safety also means that family members and kin are accorded dignity and respect (Ramsden, 1997), as well as being actively encouraged to participate in decision making with service providers about the futures of their child(ren). Ideas of cultural safety are applicable beyond considerations of race. Carers are increasingly confronted with drug-misusing families whose sub-cultural frames of reference are perhaps very dissonant from those of most workers. It can be too easy to denigrate such parents and to fail to accord them suitable dignity and respect.

Cultural safety and security begins with a state of mind. It involves entering into rhythmic interactions that engage, where possible, at a pace determined by children, young people and their family members. It requires a bi-cultural exchange between my culture and yours. Multi-cultural practices provide little guidance for direct action other than to offer a general list of principles, or so-called standards of competence. If action is required to ensure that a child or young person is made safe or because they are a threat to others, it is still essential that they be helped to process and make sense of information pertaining to their own personal circumstances, and the meaning of events that may be occurring beyond their control. Helping young people to make sense of what is happening in their lives must be done in terms that have meaning for them, using words and a language they understand.

Children's rights

Children's rights have, increasingly, become a policy focus in terms of how the state thinks about children and childhood. Specifically, rights perspectives are identified as encouraging children's participation and allowing their voices to be heard. The idea of individuals having rights can be traced back to the Enlightenment, although wider international treaties to identify and safeguard rights which inform our current thinking about rights are of more recent vintage.

The optimism that characterised the post-Second World War years saw an upsurge in interest in human rights. This culminated in the 1948 Universal Declaration of Human Rights (UDHR), which stated that: 'All human beings are born free and equal in dignity and rights. They are endowed with reason and conscience and should act towards one another in a spirit of brotherhood'. Reference to ideas of brotherhood emphasise a spirit of connectedness among human beings, adults and children alike.

These more general rights perspectives came to be applied to children and were enshrined in the 1989 United Nations Convention on the Rights of the Child (UNCRC), a legally binding treaty in international law. The UNCRC, however, was introduced in a changed political climate – one in which the generally social democratic instincts that gave rise to the UDHR had been overtaken by neoliberal political philosophies, especially in the Anglo-American world. The dominant concern within neoliberalism is for the individual rather than for any wider sense of the interconnectedness or brotherhood of human beings or human rights (Harvey, 2005). Thus, children's rights have arguably become separated off from a wider concern for human rights, a feature of which saw the growth in advocacy groups and nongovernmental organisations arguing a case for children's rights that were often reduced to a level of legal and contractual rights. This separation of children's rights from any wider conception of human rights has contributed to a suspicion of children's rights and a reluctance to engage openly with them among many who work in residential child care. In one study of Scottish residential care, Heron and Chakrabarti argue that 'the superficiality of the rights agenda has added to the complexities and tensions permeating residential provision', and has undermined practitioner morale in the process (2002: 356).

Rights perspectives, properly thought through, ought to be of central relevance to residential child care. It may be helpful for care providers to consider some of the central tenets of the UNCRC. Within it, there are four basic human rights principles meant to help with interpreting the Convention as a whole: non-discrimination (Article 2); best interests of the child (Article 3); the right to life, survival and development (Article 6) and the views of the child (Article 12) (see Mitchell, 2005). The ways in which these four principles work together can be argued to offer a rights-based approach for practitioners to apply the central idea of 'best interests', in combination with anti-discriminatory practice, respect for physical and cognitive development, and the right of young people freely to express their views. Of course, good residential care workers want to ensure children's best interests and that they are safe and are not discriminated against. They also know that, notwithstanding adult responsibility to care for children in line with their age and capacity, children and young people are themselves primary sources for information regarding adult interpretations of their best interests and can be active partners in their own care management.

Understandings of children's rights, however, have become politicised in recent years, reflecting the changing climate in which rights talk exists. Butler and Drakeford claim that in a UK context, wider understandings of rights have been hijacked by 'the far less emancipatory paradigm of child protection' (2005: 218). This places adults rather than children themselves in control of what is deemed to be a child's best interests. There are times, of course, when this has to be the case to ensure appropriate safety and decision making, but when a child protection mindset is the dominant one, it can act to exclude other possible ways of thinking of children as active constructers or co-constructors with valued adults in their own life trajectories.

As the dominance of child protection threatens the appropriate realisation of rights perspectives, so too does the increasing appropriation of rights within a consumerist model. Rights-based understandings of participation increasingly elide and have become confused with managerial and consumerist ideas (Pinkney, 2011). What is imagined is the citizen consumer rather than the relational citizen. Thus, in residential care we have statements of rights, complaints procedures, children's rights workers and independent advocates, all of which and whom can encourage children and young people to think of rights as divorced from responsibilities and relationships.

For children's rights to attain any meaningful purchase in residential child care, understandings are required that go beyond the procedural to encompass a way of thinking about children (Petrie et al, 2006), within which noble ideals of participation, inclusion and non-discrimination become central to how adults and young people engage rather than merely statements or aspirations in a policy document. Though principles might be 'enshrined in law and protocol, they can, in the final analysis, only ever be expressed meaningfully in human relationships. In other words it is only relationships that can move them beyond being an idea in print and turn them into an experienced reality' (Hennessey, 2011: 3).

Participation

Ideas about involving pupils in aspects of the running of a school or home actually have a fairly long history in the field of residential child care. An active student council, based around democratic principles, was a central feature in A. S. Neill's free school, Summerhill, from the 1920s onwards, reflecting a belief that an early experience of democracy was crucial to its later exercise by citizens.

Interest in children's rights began to emerge in residential child care over the course of the 1960s and 1970s. The focus of such interest was, primarily, on listening to children. The kind of school councils evident in schools such as Summerhill provided a template for similar models of participation across the approved school system. In some residential schools, pupils were centrally involved in appointing staff during the 1970s. At one level this was indicative of a wider ideological shift to listen to children more; at a more pragmatic level it reflected an appreciation of the benefit of 'doing with or alongside' children rather than 'doing to' of 'for' them.

We have noted that ideas of participation are central to children's rights perspectives. At a wider level, participation has become a central political consideration. Participation can operate at different levels, however. An often used model for thinking about its different levels is provided by Arnstein's (1969) ladder of citizen participation. Arnstein's ladder proceeds through 8 steps (rungs) from manipulation of citizens (1) through consultation (4) to citizen control (8), the general direction moving from non-involvement, through tokenism, to citizen power. Many attempts to involve children in residential care probably happen on the lower rungs of this ladder and tokenism is all too common.

On the other hand, critics of the ladder of participation, (Tritter and McCallum, 2006) question the fact that citizen control is held up as the 'goal' of participation. This does not always fit with participants' own reasons for engaging in decision making, within which processes they may be content with lower levels of participation, depending on the nature of the event or experience. In this regard, it is important to recognise that children and parents are not homogeneous groups and that differences in age, race, culture and ability will have implications for the level and nature of their involvement with care services. Again, what is important is the acknowledgement that there ought to be a sense of partnership between workers and young people and/or their family members, in which a young person has some of the power. A worker needs to be aware of the power differentials within any professional relationship and thus to treat other participants in the process with respect within a context of human rights. This counts for children, young people and adults (Gallagher, 2010).

Such a view of human rights is consonant with some of the foundational instruments for human rights which focus on the promotion of a sense of community in the grandest sense of that term. The ultimate goal of the UNCRC is towards:

> establishment of communities in which children *feel* that they are treated like people who count and in which their functions and opportunities in community life naturally evolve and expand. The expectation is that children's interactions take place in a context in which the adults in their lives, especially their parents, are also treated like people by public authorities, so that the institutions at the heart of society are strengthened as centers of community. (Melton, 2008: 910)

Recognition of children's rights within such an orientation does not imply that others' rights become less important. Rather, an appropriate rights consciousness 'both reflects and stimulates a culture of caring and reciprocity' (Melton, 2008: 910).

Children's involvement in social work decision making

Despite wide-ranging efforts to promote their participation in decision making, children do not always feel included. There remains a tension as to whether ideas of participation primarily serve the needs of welfare organisations, or really empower young people to shape the services they receive (Gunn, 2008). Petrie (2011) identifies proper communication with children as encouraging democratic dialogue and allowing different perspectives to be expressed and listened to. This requires a particular mindset in respect of how adults interact with children rather than a set of policy injunctions around participation.

For participation to be effective there needs to be clarity about what is expected and involved. McLeod (2006), for example, shows that while

social workers reported making efforts to listen to children and enable their
participation, very few young people felt that their views had been heard
and taken into consideration. Young people tend to understand listening
to include acting in response to what has been heard, while social workers
tended to understand listening as a receptive attitude involving respect,
openness and attentiveness. Many attempts to engage young people can feel,
and indeed may well be, tokenistic. Merely telling children that they can
attend a child in care review or care planning meeting and that their voices
are important is not going to mean much if their voices are subsequently
ignored. Organisational culture is of relevance here: properly listening to
children is less likely in hierarchical, bureaucratic and risk-averse professional
cultures. As Leeson notes:

> There is an anxiety to protect children from making mistakes, from
> making the wrong decisions. This fits with the nature of current
> social work practice being risk-averse, but leads to serious questions
> about why children are being denied the right to make mistakes,
> draw their own conclusions and learn, or even to have the right to
> change their minds. (2007: 274)

The importance of good relationships

Not surprisingly, a review of research on children's participation (Gallagher,
2010) suggests that good, long-term relationships with social workers are
crucial to children's involvement in decision making. A number of studies
have highlighted that continuity of relationships is important for looked
after children, but that frequent changes of social worker are common.
Young people and social workers report having insufficient time to build
good relationships (McLeod, 2007).

   In the context of children's participation in residential care, Holland (2009),
developing an ethics of care perspective, argues that everyday acts of care
are more important than formal statements about standards and procedural
requirements in how children experience care and the extent to which they
feel involved in the care they receive. This finding, suggesting the relative
importance of a care vis-à-vis a justice or procedural perspective, may be
thought to echo Eleanor Roosevelt's observations on the UDHR, when
asked where rights perspectives might be found. She answered:

> 'In small places, close to home – so close and so small that they
> cannot be seen on any maps of the world. Yet they are the world
> of the individual person; the neighbourhood he lives in; the school
> or college he attends; the factory, farm or office where he works.

Such are the places where every man, woman, and child seeks equal justice, equal opportunity, equal dignity without discrimination. Unless these rights have meaning there, they have little meaning anywhere. Without concerned citizen action to uphold them close to home, we shall look in vain for progress in the larger world.'

What we advocate here is a conception of children's rights that 'starts at home' and is realised through the relationships that exist within communities where adults and children come together.

Social capital

The idea of social capital has attracted much interest in recent years and may provide a helpful framework to help to understand how children and young people can become accepted within and draw strength from family and community bonds. Social capital is associated with the work of three main theorists: the French social scientist Bourdieu and the Americans Putnam and Coleman, each with a slightly different take and focus on the theme (see Field, 2003). Social capital is described by Putnam as the '… features of social life – networks, norms and trust – that enable participants to act together more effectively to pursue shared objectives' (Putnam 1995: 56). Specifically, it is used by youth justice practitioners to consider the strengths of community support a young person might harness to help them desist from offending (Whyte, 2009). It is also a lens utilised by educationalists to understand children and young people's relationships and networks, and how these are implicated in their performance in and out of school (Allen and Catts, 2012).

A social capital lens provides an antidote to linear, instrumental and bureaucratic ways of thinking about how the world operates. It operates from a broadly strengths-based perspective, based on the central premise that relationships matter: people connect through a series of networks and tend to share common values with other members of these networks. To the extent that these networks constitute a resource and provide access to a range of opportunities, they can be seen as forming a kind of capital, in a similar way that money can. Social capital is, according to Jack and Jordan, (1999) 'the trust that enables people to make contracts rather than the contracts themselves; the teamwork that makes groups function effectively rather than the roles and structures of the groups; the culture through which citizens understand and participate in politics rather than the processes of government or elections' (1999). In that sense, it is what goes on below the surface to allow things to happen. Making the most of social capital requires perhaps an element of what Bourdieu calls 'habitus' – a sort of instinctive 'feel for the game' – whereby individuals understand, negotiate and get the most out of the environment around them.

In general, the more people you know and the more you share a common outlook with them, the richer you are in social capital (Field, 2003). The implications of this are not always benign. As Bourdieu points out, social capital can act to exclude and can be associated with 'old school tie' type networks. Social capital perspectives can also be argued to mask the structural determinants of poverty and disadvantage. Even so, it is important to be aware of how social capital might accrue and act to maximise it for children and young people in the care system, who frequently lack family and community links that open doors for them which other children count upon.

Communities where higher levels of social capital are evident and where norms of trust and reciprocity are apparent – irrespective of comparable levels of economic deprivation – enjoy better health and welfare outcomes. Similarly, education outcomes can vary depending on school ethos, levels of trust, expectation and common values, a finding demonstrated in Coleman's (1988) work on Catholic schools. This question of ethos might have important implications in respect of residential child care, where the ethos of a residential home might fundamentally affect the outcomes for children and young people placed there. An ethos that sets high expectations, where staff members advocate on behalf of and take the part of young people, and where opportunities exist for a range of interests and activities, is more likely to provide an environment rich in social capital.

Social capital operates at three levels: bonding, bridging and linking. 'Bonding social capital' is characterised by strong bonds among group members: this is valuable in building a sense of shared identity and security. Families may create strong bonds, and these may be very supportive, but they may also put pressure on a young person to conform to family expectations. Bonding social capital may be seen to operate in residential care settings, where Emond (2004) identifies the close and supportive relationships that can exist within resident groups. On the other hand, bonding social capital may be apparent in disruptive behaviour among groups of residents. The concept of bonding social capital might suggest that residential workers consider the role of the resident group but also identify family bonds that might encourage positive values and aspirations. Ainsworth (2006) and Burford and Hudson (2000) have clearly shown how family participation in decision making results in better long-term outcomes for children placed in state care.

'Bridging social capital' helps people to build relationships with a wider, more varied set of people than those in the immediate family or school environment. It helps people to 'get on' and not just 'get by' (Catts and Ozga, 2005). It can be important in helping employment and career advancement. Parents seeking part-time or full-time employment for their adolescent children are often able to call upon friends or acquaintances to offer an opening. They may call upon connections to get their child into a particular football team or involve them in activities that will bring them to associate with a particular circle of friends. Children and young people in residential care often cannot rely on the same connections through their families. In that sense, there may be a role for workers to draw on their personal networks in the same way that parents do to create openings and opportunities to children from care settings.

'Linking social capital' enables connections between people across differences in status; for example, links between parents of children attending the same school but from different backgrounds, or between their children. Linking social capital connects individuals and agencies or services that they would not otherwise access easily (Catts and Ozga, 2005). In family settings, sporting and artistic activities or organisations like the Scouts or Guides can provide a vehicle for children from different social backgrounds to come together. Adults who are involved in running such activities are generally supportive of children in care. Supporting their children to participate in particular activities can require considerable investment on the part of parents, particularly in respect of ensuring travelling arrangements for training sessions or rehearsals. Residential workers should consider how they might link children and young people into different layers of community activity and involvement, and ensure that they are enabled to stick at it and not allow logistical obstacles such as staff availability or transport to get in the way. While these may pose real difficulties, parents who want the best for their children will overcome them, and it should fall on residential staff to do likewise.

Summary

Once again, this chapter leads us to (re)assert the importance of relationships in matters such as children's rights and participation. Ideas of anti-discriminatory practice and of rights should not stand as abstract principles but only achieve meaning in relationships. An appropriate framework for such relationally based practice needs to emphasise an understanding of rights that goes beyond the procedural to incorporate ideas of social connectedness and relationships between adults. It reinforces the idea of supporting children, where the adult can act as a guide, ally and mentor through whom a child can acquire increasing knowledge and competencies to take his or her place as a full member of society.

Returning to the scenario

The scenario identifies a well-functioning community meeting where initial misgivings about the ability of children and young people to chair and manage meetings have been worked through and children have risen to the challenge of doing so. There is evidence of a developing cultural, structural and practical embedding of the council idea within the ethos of the home. Anwar feels able to raise an important issue for discussion – one involving recruitment of staff, from which young people are generally excluded, or included only in a fairly tokenistic way. Jean, somewhat grudgingly at first, accepts that Anwar and the other boys in the home may actually have a legitimate point about there not being any male staff to whom they might turn. Given such responsibility, children will generally exercise it in ways that encourage a sense of community. The example given is one of a formal community meeting. In many instances the same purpose can be served more naturalistically through groups of adults and children engaging in discussion over the dinner table.

Thoughts for practice

You might open up a discussion about children's rights within your staff group. What do people think is meant by children's rights? What do they feel about children's rights? How are rights perspectives incorporated into care practices within the home?

Think about what considerations inform your approach to working with boys and girls in the home. Do you offer activities or experiences that might 'fit' with the particular needs of boys and girls? And what might be the implications of the gender composition of your staff group in framing appropriate responses?

To what extent are young people invited to participate in conversations about daily and weekly planning, about family members, school and work activities, and about holidays?

As appropriate, include young people in residence group and community activities (such as church, Scouts, Cadets or a sports club).

Maybe attend a community activity in a cultural group different from your own so that young people learn to appreciate different ways of being in the world.

Nurture opportunities for a young person to be included as part of a birth family and extended family members with whom they share a social inheritance.

Think about how you actively listen to and respond to the views of young people. How are the views of young people heard in formal meetings? How do the young people feel these opportunities work for them? Might there be less formal but more effective ways of listening to children, perhaps through discussions that happen around the table at the end of meals?

What family and community connections do children that you know have, and what doors might these open for them? How do these compare with the connections available to the children and young people in looked after and accommodated care in your home? In what ways might you 'pull some strings' for these young people?

Further reading

A useful work that social capital lens to children's networks and supports is:

Allen, J. and Catts, R. (2012) *Social capital, children and young people: implications for practice, policy and research*, Bristol: The Policy Press.

Sally Holland addresses some of the tensions between justice-based approaches to concepts such as rights and what children want in their everyday experiences of care:

Holland, S. (2009) 'Looked after children and the ethic of care', *British Journal of Social Work*, vol 40, no 6, pp 1664–80.

Melton offers a sensible account of children's rights located within a concern for human rights more generally:

Melton, G. (2008) 'Beyond balancing: toward an integrated approach to children's rights', *Journal of Social Issues*, vol 64, no 4, pp 903–20.

Conclusion

We have sought in this book to provide an account of residential child care that reflects the complexity of everyday practice and that locates this practice within a broad theoretical context. We are aware, though, that the wider climate within which such practice takes place is often not conducive to the provision of quality care. External omens are not good; perceived as an expensive and not a particularly effective service, residential child care will be further squeezed financially. The push towards marketing and privatising services, with all that entails in terms of reducing costs and lowering qualifications, is likely to continue apace.

Within social work, residential child care has been subject to a persistent ambivalence, faced with many detractors and only lukewarm defenders. At the heart of this ambivalence, which has been and continues to be evident in social work, is a failure of that profession to properly appreciate concepts of care giving and receiving. At one level, this failure to appreciate the nature and importance of care has been manifest in a search for theoretical rationales for residential child care that are grounded primarily in the discipline of psychology. While some psychological theories provide helpful insights into the practice of residential child care, they rarely capture its breadth and intricacy in the everyday practices of care. Developments in positive psychology notwithstanding, these theories also tend to locate practice at the level of individual children's problems rather than being motivated by a wider moral purpose to promote their growth, flourishing and happiness.

Other trends within social work (and within public service provision more generally) have seen a drive towards more outcome driven services within increasingly managerial cultures. A consequence of this is that care has been reconceptualised as a technical/rational task, amenable to a range of short-term targets and performance indicators, rather than the moral, practical and relational endeavour we have attempted to document in this book. The outside world speaks in what the care ethics literature would identify as a justice voice (Gilligan, 1993), emphasising a language of risk, rights, protection, best practice, evidence, standards and inspection. This justice voice tends to 'crowd out a care voice that struggles to murmur of love, connection and control' (Steckley and Smith, 2011: 191).

Ironically, the regulatory infrastructures established with the stated intention of improving services contribute towards their ever-increasing bureaucratisation. We are landed with the wrong kind of regulation – what Jordan (2010) calls contractual rather than moral regulation. Contractual regulation assumes that care can be set down in a series of standards, registration requirements, service level agreements and external monitoring of these, rather than face-to-face contact between the cared for and those caring, with all the messiness and moral ambiguity that such encounters entail.

Excessive regulation risks shifting the focus of everyday caring away from the level of human contact, towards meeting procedural demands of an entrenched inspectorial apparatus. This is philosophically problematic because, as we have already suggested, bureaucracy distances us from the subjects of our care. By such reckoning, the plethora of rules and regulations that increasingly surround practice are not just minor but necessary irritants; they serve to dull moral impulses to care and to 'be for' those with whom we work (Smith, 2011b: 3). Rehabilitation of the concept of care within professional discourses might, according to Meagher and Parton, provide 'a key counterweight to the increasing processes of managerialisation' (2004: 4).

Despite the inhospitable external environment, residential child care continues and will continue to care for some of society's most disadvantaged children and young people. And there are some beacons of hope with respect to how it might do so, in the academic literature, at least. Bondi et al question dominant notions of professionalism and 'whether the knowledge or rational judgement required for the effective conduct of caring or people professions is reducible to the technical "evidence-based" rationality to which modern professions as medicine seem sometimes to have aspired'. They further doubt whether 'either social or natural science is well-placed to determine the goals of human welfare and flourishing' (2011: 2). Smith and Smith suggest that 'Bureaucratic professionalism may well be working itself into a corner. We hope more will have the courage to develop spaces where helping is on a human scale' (2008: 154). By its very nature, residential child care needs to be enacted daily on a human scale.

Such a human scale also demands that we consider care outcomes in a different light, locating these not in the managerial grand strategies of key performance indicators but in the small things and developmental achievements that may not be immediately apparent to those wishing to measure care with coffee spoons. Real success is measured in the everyday successes and achievements of children and young people. An experienced residential school manager captured this in a conference presentation, noting that:

> Whether we see ourselves as 'pedagogues', 'upbringers', 'experience arrangers' or 'child and youth care workers' we all understand the powerful therapeutic value of ordinary life events. Our successes are:

- the child who learns to tie their laces;
- the child who wakes up rested without having had a nightmare;
- the child who manages a night without a wet bed;
- the child who begins using a knife and fork;
- the child who manages to ride their bike;
- the child who starts to improve their reading;
- the child who takes part in the school Christmas show;
- the child who copes with a visit from their parent;
- the child who builds the confidence to be part of the school council;
- the child choosing to help clear the snow;
- the child taking part in the football game;
- the child gaining qualification;.
- the child attending Brownies, Guides, Boys' Brigade or Scouts;
- The child learning to swim. (Gibson, 2011)

Successful care outcomes depend on the process as much as on any measurable end product of professional involvement. If the nature and process of involvement is right then outcomes are likely to be better: it is difficult to disentangle the two. The way in which care is offered needs to be infused with a moral purpose. Webb's (2010) identification of the insidious leniencies that pervade current day child care provides a damning indictment of a system that has lost its way. Care workers need to be able to reclaim a belief that they can make a difference in the lives of children and, as corporate parents, can provide them with the same love, control and aspirations that any good parent would want for their children. Currently, this happens in only patchy ways and often in spite of, rather than because of, the system (DCSF, 2009).

While it ought to be purposeful, child and youth care is not necessarily predictable. Magnuson reminds us that 'development and growth is a mysterious, asynchronous, non-linear process and dynamic. All child and youth care work aims to further growth and change, yet its pedagogy is not interventionist and direct ... [but] indirect, cooperative, collaborative and invitational' (2003: xxii–xxiii).

Residential child care practice based upon mysterious dynamics of growth and change is, of course, an anathema to 'commonsense' political and managerial systems. Existing ways of thinking are so entrenched as to become 'taken for granted'. It can be hard to question current levels of managerial control and compliance, hard to imagine a residential care system without its attendant regulatory apparatus, and hard to propose alternatives. We are, as Fielding and Moss discuss, held within a 'dictatorship of no alternatives' (2011: 1). But, they go on to argue, we need to overthrow this dictatorship and to think of different ideas of children and childhood, and of our role as adults in children's upbringing. It is a task that requires imagination – a quality that needs to be as central to the child and youth care canon as any psychological or instrumental understandings (Gharabaghi, 2008).

Alternatives to current ways of thinking will not come about if workers sit back and rely on the wider political and professional power blocks to improve care. There are encouraging signs of an emerging professional activism in both England and Scotland, where care workers are coming together within professional organisations to demand a voice in decisions made about the future of residential child care. Ireland, in this respect, already has its own professional organisation. Much of this developing practitioner interest converges around ideas of social pedagogy. Such an orientation may offer a more conducive practice paradigm than social work within which to take forward ideas on how best to care for children and young people.

References

Ainsworth, F. (1981) 'The training of personnel for group care with children', in F. Ainsworth and L.C. Fulcher (eds) *Group care for children: Concept and issues*, London: Tavistock, pp 225–47.

Ainsworth, F. (2006) 'Group care practitioners as family workers', in L. C. Fulcher and F. Ainsworth (eds) *Group care practice with children and young people revisited*, New York: The Haworth Press, pp 75–86.

Alexander, K., Entwisle, D. and Olson, L. (2001) 'Schools, achievement, and inequality: a seasonal perspective', *Educational Evaluation and Policy Analysis*, vol 23, no 2, pp 171–91.

Allen, J. and Catts, R. (2012) *Social capital, children and young people: Implications for practice, policy and research*, Bristol: The Policy Press.

Altman, B. (2002) 'Working with play', *CYC-Online*, issue 36, www.cyc-net. org/cyc-online/cycol-0102-altman.html

Andersen, L. (2009) 'On the practice of working as a milieu-therapist with children', in H. Kornerup (ed) *Milieu-therapy with children: Planned environmental therapy in Scandinavia*, Perikon, distributed London: Karnac Books, pp 67–92.

Anglin, J. (1999) 'The uniqueness of child and youth care: a personal perspective', *Child and Youth Care Forum*, vol 28, no 2, pp 143–50.

Anglin, J. (2002) *Pain, normality and the struggle for congruence: Reinterpreting residential care for children and youth*, New York: The Haworth Press.

Antonovsky, A. (1996) 'The salutogenic model as a theory to guide health promotion', *Health Promotion International*, vol 11, no 1, pp 11–18.

Arnstein, S. (1969) 'A ladder of citizen participation', *Journal of the American Institute of Planners*, vol 35, pp 216–24.

Ballard, R. (1979) 'Ethnic minorities and the social services: what type of service?', in V. S. Khan (ed) *Minority families in Britain*, London: Macmillan, pp 146–64.

Bandura, A. (1977) *Social learning theory*, New York: General Learning Press.

Baron-Cohen, S. (2008) *Autism and Asperger syndrome: The facts*, Oxford: Oxford University Press

Bauman, Z. (1993) *Postmodern ethics*, Oxford: Blackwell.

Bauman, Z. (1998) *Work, consumerism and the new poor*, Buckingham: Open University Press.

Bauman, Z. (2000) 'Special essay: am I my brother's keeper?', *European Journal of Social Work*, vol 3, no 1, pp 5–11.

Bebbington, A. and Miles, J. (1989) 'The background of children who enter local authority care', *British Journal of Social Work*, vol 19, no 1, pp 349–68.

Beedell, C. (1970) Residential Life with Children. London: Routeledge and Kegan Paul

Benenson, J. F. (2005) 'Sex differences', in B. Hopkins, R. Barr, G. Michel and P. Rochat (eds) *The Cambridge encyclopedia of child development*, Cambridge: Cambridge University Press.

Bengtsson, E., Chamberlain, C., Crimmens, D. and Stanley, J. (2008) *Introducing social pedagogy into residential child care in England: An evaluation of a project commissioned by the Social Education Trust (SET) in September 2006 and managed by the National Centre for Excellence in Residential Child Care (NCERCC)*, London: SET and NCERCC.

Berridge, D. (2006) 'Theory and explanation in child welfare: education and looked-after children', *Child and Family Social Work*, vol 12, pp 1–10.

Berridge, D. and Brodie, I. (1998) *Children's homes revisited*, London: Jessica Kingsley Publishers.

Biddulph, S. (2003) *Raising boys: why boys are different – and how to help them become happy and well-balanced men*, London: Harper Thorsons.

Bion, W. R. (1962) *Learning from experience*, London: Karnac.

Bloomer, K. (2008) *Working it out: Developing the children's sector workforce*, Edinburgh: Children in Scotland.

Boddy, J. (2011) 'The supportive relationship in public care: the relevance of social pedagogy', in C. Cameron and P. Moss (eds) *Social pedagogy and working with children and young people: Where care and education meet*, London: Jessica Kingsley Publishers, pp 105–24.

Bondi, L., Carr, D., Clark, C. and Clegg, C. (2011) *Towards professional wisdom: Practical deliberation in the people professions*, Farnham: Ashgate.

Boud, D. and Falchikov, N. (2007) *Rethinking assessment for higher education: Learning for the longer term*, Routledge: London.

Bourdieu, P. (1984) *Distinction: A social critique of the judgement of taste*. London, Routledge.

Bourdieu, P. (1986) 'The forms of capital'. In J G. Richardson (ed.) *Handbook of theory and research for the sociology of education*, New York: Greenwood Press pp 241-58.

Bowlby, J. (1951) *Maternal care and mental health*, Geneva: World Health Organization.

Bowlby, J. (1988) *A secure base: Clinical applications of attachment theory*, London: Routledge.

Brannen, J. and Moss, P. (eds) (2003) *Rethinking children's care*, Buckingham: Open University Press.

Brendtro, L. and du Toit, L. (2005) *Response ability pathways: Restoring bonds of respect*, Cape Town: Pre Text Publishers.

Brendtro, L., Brokenleg, M. and Van Bockern, S. (2002) *Reclaiming youth at risk: Our hope for the future*, Bloomington, IN: Solution Tree.

Brokenleg, M (1999) *Native American perspectives on generosity*, www.altruists. org/f164

Bronfenbrenner, U. (1979) *The ecology of human development*, Cambridge, MA: Harvard University Press.

Burford, G. and Casson, S. (1989) 'Including families in residential work: educational and agency tasks', *British Journal of Social Work*, vol 19, no 1, pp 19–37.

Burford, G. and Hudson, J. (eds) (2000) *Family group conferences: New directions in community-centered child and family practice*, New York: Aldine de Gruyter.

Burmeister, E. (1960) *The professional houseparent*, New York: Columbia University Press,

Butler, I. and Drakeford, M. (2005) *Scandal, social policy and social welfare*, Bristol: BASW/The Policy Press.

Cameron, C. (2003) 'An historical perspective on changing child care policy', in J. Brannan and P. Moss (eds) *Rethinking children's care*, Buckingham: Open University Press, pp 80-95.

Cameron, C. and Moss, P. (eds) (2011) *Social pedagogy and working with children and young people: Where care and education meet*, London: Jessica Kingsley Publishers.

Cameron, R.J. and McGinn, C. (2008) 'The authentic warmth dimension of professional childcare', *British Journal of Social Work*, 8(6): 1151-72.

Catts, R. and Ozga, J. (2005) *What is social capital and how might it be used in Scotland's schools?* Briefing paper, www.ces.ed.ac.uk/PDF%20Files/Brief036.pdf

Centre for Social Justice (2008) *Breakthrough Glasgow: Ending the costs of social breakdown*, www.centreforsocialjustice.org.uk/client/downloads/BreakthroughGlasgow.pdf

Children in Scotland (2008) *Making the gender equality duty real for children, young people and their fathers*, Edinburgh: Children in Scotland.

Celcis (Centre for Excellence for Looked After Children in Scotland) (2010) 'Go outdoors: guidance and good practice on encouraging outdoor activities in residential care', www.celcis.org/resources/entry/go_outdoors_guidance_and_good_practice_on_encouraging_outdoor_activities

Clarke, J. and Newman, J. (1997) *The managerial state: power, politics and ideology in the remaking of social welfare*, London: Sage Publications.

Clough, P. and Nutbrown, C. (2005) 'Inclusion and development in the early years: making inclusion conventional?', *Child Care in Practice*, vol 11, no 2, pp 99–102.

Clough, R., Bullock, R. and Ward, A. (2006) *What works in residential child care? A review of research evidence and the practical considerations*, London: National Children's Bureau.

Cockburn, T. (2005) 'Children and the feminist ethic of care', *Childhood*, vol 12, pp 71–89.

Coleman, J. (1988) 'Social capital in the creation of human capital', *American Journal of Sociology*, supplement 94, pp 95–120.

Connelly, G., McKay, E., and O'Hagan, P. (2003) *Learning with care: information for carers, social workers and teachers concerning the education of looked after children and young people*, Glasgow: University of Strathclyde/HMIE/SWSI.

Corby, B., Doig, A. and Roberts, V. (2001) *Public inquiries into abuse of children in residential care*, London: Jessica Kingsley Publishers.

Costa, M. and Walter, C. (2006) 'Care: the art of living', in R. Jackson (ed) *Holistic special education: Camphill principles and practice*, Edinburgh: Floris Books.

Courtney, M. E. and Iwaniec, D. (2009) *Residential care of children: comparative perspectives*, New York: Oxford University Press.

Cree, V. and Davis, A. (2007) *Social work: voices from the inside*, Abingdon: Routledge.

Cree, V.E. and Wallace, S.J. (2005) 'Risk and protection' in Adams, R., Payne, M. and Dominelli, (eds) *Social work futures*, Basingstoke: Palgrave Macmillan: 115-127.

Cross, C. (2008) 'Resolutions', *Goodenoughcaring e-journal*, www. goodenoughcaring.com/JournalArticle.aspx?cpid=73

Daniel, B., Featherstone, B., Hooper, C. A. and Scourfield, J. (2005) 'Why gender matters for Every Child Matters', *British Journal of Social Work*, vol 35, no 8, pp 1343–55.

Davidson, J., McCullough, D., Steckley, L. and Warren, T. (2005) *Holding safely*, Glasgow: Scottish Institute for Residential Child Care.

Davies, M. (ed) (2012) *Social work with children and families,* Basingstoke: Palgrave Macmillan.

DCSF (Department for Children, Schools and Families) (2009) *Looked-after children: Children, Schools and Families Committee*, www.publications. parliament.uk/pa/cm200809/cmselect/cmchilsch/111/11107.htm

Department for Education and Skills (DfES), (2003) *Every Child Matters – the Green Paper* Norwich, The Stationery Office.

de Certeau, M. (1984) *The practice of everyday life* (trans S Rendall), Berkeley, CA: University of California Press.

De Jong, P. and Kim Berg, I. (2002) *Interviewing for solutions* (2nd edn), Pacific Grove, CA: Brooks Cole Publishers.

Delano, F. and Shah, J. C. (2011) 'Games played in the supervisory relationship: the modern version', *Relational Child and Youth Care Practice*, vol 24, no 1/2, pp 177–85.

DES (Department of Education and Skills) (2006) *Care matters: Transforming the lives of children and young people in care*, Norwich: The Stationery Office.

Digney, J. (2005) 'Towards a comprehension of the roles of humour in child and youth care', *Relational Child and Youth Care Practice*, vol 18, no 4, pp 9–18.

Dimigen, G., Del Priore, C., Butler, S., Evans, S., Ferguson, L. and Swan, M. (1999) 'Psychiatric disorder among children at time of entering local authority care', *British Medical Journal*, vol 319, no 7211, p 675.

Douglas, R. and Payne, C. (1981) 'Alarm bells for the clock-on philosophy', *Social Work Today*, vol 12, no 23, pp 110-11.

Dunne, J. (1993) *Back to the rough ground: 'phronesis' and 'techne' in modern philosophy and in Aristotle*, Notre Dame, IN: Notre Dame University Press.

Eichsteller, G. and Holthoff, S. (2010) *Social pedagogy training pack*, ThemPra Social Pedagogy Community Interest Company.

Ely, P. and Denney, D. (1987) *Social work in a multi-racial society*, Aldershot, Hants: Gower.

Emond, R. (2000) 'Survival of the skilful: an ethnographic study of two groups of young people in residential care', unpublished PhD thesis, University of Stirling.

Emond, R. (2004) 'Rethinking our understanding of the resident group in group care', *Child and Youth Care Forum*, vol 33, no 3, pp 193–208.

Emond, R. (2008) 'Children's voices, children's rights', in A. Kendrick (ed) *Residential child care: prospects and challenges*, London: Jessica Kingsley Publishers, pp 183–96.

Emond, R. (2010) 'Caring as a moral, practical and powerful endeavour: peer care in a Cambodian orphanage', *British Journal of Social Work*, vol 40, no 1, pp 63–81.

Entwistle, H. (1979) *Antonio Gramsci: conservative schooling for radical politics*, London: Routledge and Kegan Paul.

Fanshel, D., Finch, S. J. and Grundy, J. F. (1990) *Foster children in life course perspective*, New York: Colombia University Press.

Ferguson, I. (2008) 'Neoliberalism, happiness and well-being', *International Socialism*, vol 117, pp 87–121.

Fewster, G. (1991) 'Editorial: the selfless professional', *Journal of Child and Youth Care*, vol 6, no 4, pp 69–72.

Fewster, G. (2005) 'Just between you and me: personal boundaries in professional relationships', *Relational Child and Youth Care Practice*, vol 18, no 2, pp 7–14. delete

Field, J. (2003) *Social capital*, London: Routledge.

Fielding, M. and Moss, P. (2011) *Radical education and the common school*, Abingdon: Routledge.

Fisher, B. and Tronto, J. (1990) 'Toward a feminist theory of caring', in F. Abel and M. Nelson (eds) *Circles of care*, Albany: State University of New York, pp 35–62.

Forrester, D. (2008) 'Is the care system failing children?', *The Political Quarterly*, vol 79, no 2, pp 206–11.

Forrester, D., Goodman, K., Cocker, C., Binnie, C. and Jensch, G. (2009) 'What is the impact of public care on children's welfare? A review of research findings from England and Wales and their policy implications', *Journal of Social Policy*, vol 38, no 3, pp 439–56.

Frampton, P. (2004) *The golly in the cupboard*, Manchester: Tamic Publications.

Francis, J. (2006) 'Could do better! Supporting the education of looked-after children', in A. Kendrick (ed) *Residential child care: prospects and challenges*, London: Jessica Kingsley Publishers.

Freire, P. (1972) *Pedagogy of the oppressed*, Harmondsworth: Penguin.

Fulcher, L. C. (1993) 'Yes Henry, the space we create does indeed control us!', *Journal of Child and Youth Care*, vol 8, no 2, pp 91–100.

Fulcher, L. C. (1997) 'Changing care in a changing world: the old and new worlds', *Social Work Review*, vol 9, no 1/2, pp 20–6.

Fulcher, L. C. (1998) 'Acknowledging culture in child and youth care practice', *Social Work Education*, vol 17, no 3, pp 321–38.

Fulcher, L. C. (2001) 'Differential assessment of residential group care for children and young people', *The British Journal of Social Work*, vol 31, no 3, pp 415–34.

Fulcher, L. C. (2002) 'Cultural safety and the duty of care', *Child Welfare*, vol 81, no 5, pp 689–708.

Fulcher, L. C. (2003) 'Rituals of encounter that guarantee cultural safety', *Journal of Relational Child and Youth Care Practice*, vol 16, no 3, pp 20–7, www.cyc-net.org/lz/a-3-2.html

Fulcher, L. C. (2005) 'The soul, rhythms and blues of responsive child and youth care at home or away from home', *Child and Youth Care*, vol 27, no 1/2, pp 27–50.

Fulcher, L. C. and Ainsworth, F. (eds) (2006) *Group care practice with children and young people revisited*, New York: The Haworth Press.

Fulcher, L. C. and Garfat, T. (2008) *Quality care in a family setting: a practical guide for foster carers*, Cape Town: Pretext.

Furedi, F. (2003) *Therapy culture: cultivating vulnerability in an uncertain age*, London: Routledge.

Furedi, F. (2009) *Wasted: Why education isn't educating*, London: Continuum Press.

Gallagher, B. (2000) 'The extent and nature of known cases of institutional child sex abuse', *British Journal of Social Work*, vol 30, pp 795–817.

Gallagher, M (2010) 'Literature review 2: children and families', Engaging with Involuntary Service Users in Social Work, www.socialwork.ed.ac. uk/esla/resources/publications

Garfat, T. (1998) 'The effective child and youth care intervention: a phenomenological inquiry', *Journal of Child and Youth Care*, special edition, vol 12, no 1/2.

Garfat, T. (1999) 'Editorial: hanging-in', *CYC-Online*, issue 9, www.cyc-net. org/cyc-online/cycol-1099-editor.html

Garfat, T. (2001) 'Developmental stages of child and youth care workers: an interactional perspective', *The International Child and Youth Care Network*, issue 24, www.cyc-net.org/cyc-online/cycol-0101-garfat.html

Garfat, T. (2002) *The use of everyday events in child and youth care work*, www. cyc-net.org/cyc-online/cycol-0402-garfat.html

Garfat, T. (2007) 'The supervision connection', *CYC-Online*, issue 96, www. cyc-net.org/cyc-online/cycol-0107-supervision.html

Garfat, T. and Fulcher, L. C. (2011) 'Characteristics of a child and youth care approach', *Journal of Relational Child and Youth Care Practice*, vol 24, no 1/2, p 7.

Gharabaghi, K. (2008) 'Contemplations about the imagination and complacency in child and youth care practice', *Relational Child and Youth Care Practice vol* 21, no 4, pp 30–42.

Gharabaghi, K. (2011) 'A culture of education: enhancing school performance of youth living in residential group care in Ontario', *Child Welfare*, vol 90, no 1, pp 75–91.

Gharabaghi, K. (2012) 'Translating evidence into practice: supporting the school performance of young people living in residential group care in Ontario', *Children and Youth Services Review*, doi:10.1016/j. childyouth.2012.01.038.

Gibson, D. (2011) 'Plenary presentation' to *Celebrating Success in Residential Child Care conference*, Scottish Government, Glasgow, 22nd March.

Gill, T. (2007) *No fear: growing up in a risk averse society*, London: Calouste Gulbenkian Foundation.

Gill, T. (2010) *Nothing ventured… balancing risks and benefits in the outdoors*, English Outdoor Council, www.englishoutdoorcouncil.org/wp-content/ uploads/Nothing-Ventured.pdf.

Gilligan, C. (1993) *In a different voice: Psychological theory and women's development*, Cambridge, MA: Harvard University Press.

Glasser, W. (1969) Schools without failure, New York : Harper and Row

Glasser, W. D. (1998) *Choice theory: A new psychology of personal freedom*, New York: HarperCollins.

Goffman, E. (1968) *Asylums*, Harmondsworth: Penguin.

Goldson, B. (2002) 'New Labour, social justice and children: political calculation and the deserving–undeserving schism', *British Journal of Social Work*, vol 32, pp 683–95.

Grant, A., Ennis, J. and Stuart, F. (2002) 'Looking after health: a joint working approach to improving the health outcomes of looked after and accommodated children and young people', *Scottish Journal of Residential Child Care*, vol 1, no 1, pp 23-30.

Green, L. and Masson, H. (2002) 'Adolescents who sexually abuse and residential accommodation: issues of risk and vulnerability', *British Journal of Social Work*, vol 32, no 2, pp 149–68.

Gunn, R. (2008) The power to shape decisions? An exploration of young people's power in participation', *Health and Social Care in the Community*, 16(3), 253-261

Halvorsen, A. (2009) 'What counts in child protection and welfare?', *Qualitative Social Work*, vol 8, no 1, pp 65–82.

Hanlon, P. and Carlisle, S. (2010) 'Dis-ease, the modern epidemic: 2.2 depression – a rising tide?', www.afternow.co.uk/images/downloads/pdfs/2.2%20Depression%20-%20a%20rising%20tide.pdf

Hanlon, P., Carlisle, S. and Henderson, G. (2011) 'Consumerism, dissatisfaction guaranteed: 3.6 influences on well-being', www.phru.net/mhin/childandyouth/Lists/Announcements/Attachments/65/Influences%20on%20well-being.pdf

Hanlon, P., Carlisle, S., Lyon, A., Hannah, M. and Reilly, D. (2011) 'Dis-ease, the modern epidemic: 2.4 drugs, addiction and the ingenuity gap', www.afternow.co.uk/images/downloads/pdfs/2.4%20Drugs,%20addiction%20and%20the%20ingenuity%20gap.pdf

Harvey, D. (2005) *A brief history of neoliberalism*, Oxford: Oxford University Press.

Head, J. (1999) *Understanding the boys: Issues of behaviour and achievement*, London: Psychology Press.

Heckenlaible-Gotto, M. (2006) 'Editorial: from problems to strengths', *Reclaiming Children and Youth*, vol 15, no 3, pp 130–1, www.cyc-net.org/Journals/rcy-15-3.html deleteHeimler, E. (1975) *Survival in society*, London: Weidenfeld and Nicholson.

Held, V. (2006) *The ethics of care: Personal, political and global*, Oxford: Oxford University Press.

Hennessey, R. (2011) *Relationship skills in social work*, London: Sage.

Heron, G. and Chakrabarti, M. (2002) 'Examining the perceptions and attitudes of staff working in community based children's homes', *Qualitative Social Work*, vol 1, no 3, pp 341–58.

Hewitt, P. (2003) *The looked-after kid: Memoirs from the children's home*, Edinburgh: Mainstream Publishing.

Hill, M., Walker, M., Moodie, K., Wallace, B., Bannister, J., Khan, F., McIvor, G. and Kendrick, A. (2005) *Fast track children's hearings pilot: Final report of the evaluation of the pilot*, Edinburgh: University of Strathclyde/University of Glasgow/University of Stirling/Scottish Executive.

Hoffman, M. 2000. *Empathy and moral development*, Cambridge: Cambridge University Press.

Holland, S. (2009) 'Looked after children and the ethic of care', *British Journal of Social Work*, vol 40, no 6, pp 1664–80.

Holman, B. (1998) *Child care revisited: The children's departments 1948–1971*, London: ICSE.

Horwath, J. (2000) 'Childcare with gloves on: protecting children and young people in residential care', *British Journal of Social Work*, vol 30, pp 179–91.

Howe, D. (1995) *Attachment theory for social work practice*, Basingstoke: Macmillan.

Howe, D. (2005) *Child abuse and neglect: Attachment, development and intervention*, Basingstoke: Palgrave Macmillan.

Hughes, D. (2006) *Building the bonds of attachment: Awakening love in deeply troubled children*, Lanham, MD: Jason Aronson Inc.

Iacoboni, M. (2008) *Mirroring people: The new science of how we connect with others*, New York: Farrar, Straus and Giroux.

Jack, G 2010. 'Place matters: the significance of place attachments for children's well-being', *British Journal of Social Work* 40(3): 755-71.

Jack, G. and Jordan, B. (1999) 'Social capital and child welfare', *Children and Society*, vol 13, no 4, pp 242–56.

Jackson, P. (2004) 'Rights and representation in the Scottish children's hearings system', in *Meeting needs, addressing deeds: working with young people who offend*, Glasgow: NCH, pp 71-9.

Jackson, R. (2011) 'Challenges of residential and community care: "the times they are a–changin"', *Journal of Intellectual Disability Research*, vol 55, no 9, pp 933–44.

Jackson, S. (1987) *The education of children in care*, Bristol: School of Applied Social Studies, University of Bristol.

Jackson, S. (2006) 'Looking after children away from home: past and present', in E. Chase, A. Simon and S. Jackson, *In care and after: A positive perspective*, London: Routledge, pp 9–25.

Jackson, S. and Martin, P.Y. (1998) 'Surviving the care system: education and resilience', *Journal of Adolescence*, vol 21, pp 569–83.

Jackson, S. & Simon, A. (2006) The costs and benefits of educating children in care, in E. Chase, A. Simon and S. Jackson (eds) *In care and after: A positive perspective*, London: Routledge. pp.44–62.

Jackson, S., Ajayi, S. and Quigley, M. (2005) *Going to university from care*, London: Institute of Education.

Jones, J. (2010) 'Raising children: a character-based approach to residential child care', *Scottish Journal of Residential Child Care*, vol 9, no 2, pp 22–7.

Jones, R. (2009) 'In our constipated care culture, thank heavens for the rule benders', *The Guardian*, 10 February, www.guardian.co.uk/commentisfree/2009/feb/10/care-society-culture-fearwww.guardian.co.uk/commentisfree/2009/feb/10/care-society-culture-fear

Jordan, B. (2010) *Why the Third Way failed,* Bristol: The Policy Press.

Kellmer-Pringle, M. K. (1975) *The needs of children*, London: Hutchinson.

Kendrick, A. (2012) 'What research tells us about residential child care', in M. Davies (ed) *Social work with children and families*, Basingstoke: Palgrave Macmillan.

Kent, R. (1997) *Children's safeguards review*, Edinburgh: Stationery Office.

Khan, V. S. (1982) 'The role of the culture of dominance in structuring the experience of ethnic minorities', in C. Husband (ed) *Race in Britain*, London: Hutchison.

Kilbrandon, L. (1964) *The Kilbrandon Report: Children and young persons Scotland*, Edinburgh: Scottish Home and Health Department/Scottish Education Department.

Kleipoedszus, S. (2011) 'Communication and conflict: an important part of social pedagogic relationships', in C. Cameron and P. Moss (eds) *Social pedagogy and working with children and young people: Where care and education meet*, London: Jessica Kingsley Publishers, pp 125–40.

Knapp, M. (2006) 'The economics of group care practice: a re-appraisal', in L. C. Fulcher and F. Ainsworth (eds) *Group care practice with children and young people revisited*, New York: The Haworth Press, pp 259–84.

Kornerup, H. (ed) (2009) *Milieu-therapy with children: Planned environmental therapy in Scandinavia*, Perikon, distributed London: Karnac Books.

Lane, K. (2008) *Hey, Minister, leave our schools alone*, www.childrenwebmag.com/articles/education/hey-minister-leave-our-schools-alone

Lane, R. E. (2001) *The loss of happiness in market democracies*, New Haven, CT: Yale University Press.

Layard, R. (2006) *Happiness: Lessons from a new science* (2nd edn), London: Penguin.

Leeson, C. (2007) 'My life in care: experiences of non-participation in decision-making processes', *Child and Family Social Work*, vol 12, pp 268–77.

Leigh, J. W. (1998) *Communication for cultural competence*, Sydney: Allyn and Bacon.

Levitas, R. A. (1998) *The Inclusive society? Social exclusion and New Labour*, Basingstoke: Macmillan

Lewin, K. (1951) *Field theory in social science: Selected theoretical papers*, ed. D. Cartwright, New York: Harper and Row.

Lickona, T. (1983) *Raising good children: Helping your child through the stages of moral development*, Toronto: Bantam Books.

Linnane, C. (2008) 'Encouraging reading among children in care: the Edinburgh Reading Champion project', *Scottish Journal of Residential Child Care*, Special edition: Education, vol 7, no 2, pp 25–7.

Lister, R. (2003) 'Investing in the citizen-workers of the future: transformations in citizenship and the state under New Labour', *Social Policy and Administration*, vol 37, no 5, pp 427–43.

Long, N. (2007) 'The therapeutic power of kindness', *Cyc-Online*, issue 98, www.cyc-net.org/cyc-online/cycol-0307-long.html

Lonne, B., Parton, N., Thomas, J. and Harries, M. (2009) *Reforming child protection*, London; New York: Routledge. delete

Loughmiller, C. (1979) *Kids in trouble: An adventure in education*, Texas: Wildwood Books.

Lynch, K., Baker, J. and Lyons, M. (2009) *Affective equality: Love, care and injustice,* Basingstoke: Palgrave Macmillan.

McGhee, J., Mellon, M. and Whyte, B. (eds) (2004) *Meeting needs, addressing deeds: Working with young people who offend*, Glasgow: NCH.

McLaughlin K. (2010) 'The social worker versus the general social care council: an analysis of Care Standards tribunal hearings and decisions', *British Journal of Social Work*, vol.40 no.1, pp.311-327

MacLean, K. (2003) 'Resilience – what it is and how children and young people can be helped to develop it', *In Residence*, no 1, Glasgow: Scottish Institute for Residential Child Care.

McLeod, A. (2006) 'Respect or empowerment? Alternative understandings of "listening" in childcare social work', *Adoption and Fostering*, 30(4), 43-52

McLeod, A. (2007) 'Whose agenda? Issues of power and relationship when listening to looked-after young people', *Child and Family Social Work*, 12, 278-86

McLeod, A. (2010) 'A friend and an equal: do young people in care seek the impossible from their social workers?', *British Journal of Social Work*, vol 40, pp 772–88.

MacMurray, J. (2004) *Selected philosophical writings*, ed E. McIntosh, Exeter: Imprint.

McWilliam, E. (2000) 'Foreword', in R.T. Johnson *Hands off! The disappearance of touch in the care of children*, New York: Peter Lang.

Magnuson, D. (2003) 'Preface', in T. Garfat (ed) *A child and youth care approach to working with families*, New York: The Haworth Press Inc, pp xxi–xxiii.

Maier, H. W. (1979. 'The core of care: essential ingredients for the development of children at home and away from home', *Child Care Quarterly*, vol 8, pp 161-73.

Maier, H.W. (1981) 'Essential components in care and treatment environments for children', in F. Ainsworth and L.C. Fulcher (eds) *Group care for children: Concept and issues*, London: Tavistock, pp. 19-70.

Maier, H.W. (1982) 'The space we create controls us', *Residential Group Care and Treatment*, vol 1, no1, pp 51-9.

Maier, H.W. (1985) 'Primary care in secondary settings: inherent strains', in L.C. Fulcher and F. Ainsworth (eds) *Group care practice with children*, London: Tavistock.

Maier, H.W. (1987) *Developmental group care of children and youth: Concepts and practice*, New York: Haworth Press.

Maier, H.W. (1992) 'Rhythmicity: a powerful force for experiencing unity and personal connections', *Journal of Child and Youth Care Work*, vol 8, www.cyc-net.org/cyc-online/cycol-0704-rhythmicity.htm

Maier, H.W. (2000) *Establishing meaningful contacts with children and youth*, www.cyc-net.org/maier-contacts.htm

Maslow, A.H. (1943) 'Theory of human motivation', *Psychological Review*, vol 50, pp 370-96.

May, V. (2011) 'Self, belonging and social change', *Sociology*, vol 45, no 3, pp 363-78.

Meagher, G. and Parton, N. (2004) 'Modernising social work and the ethics of care', *Social Work and Society*, vol 2, no 1, pp 10–27.

Melton, G. (2008) 'Beyond balancing: toward an integrated approach to children's rights', *Journal of Social Issues*, vol 64, no 4.

Meltzer, H. (2000) *The mental health of children and adolescents in Great Britain*, London: Office of National Statistics.

Meltzer, H., Lader, D., Corbin, T., Goodman, R. and Ford, T. (2004) *The mental health of young people looked after by local authorities in Scotland*, London: The Stationery Office.

Menzies Lyth, I. (1960) 'A case-study in the functioning of social systems as a defence against anxiety', *Human Relations*, vol 13, no 2, pp 95–121, http://hum.sagepub.com/content/13/2/95.extract

Milligan, I. (1998) 'Residential child care is not social work!', *Social Work Education*, vol 17, no 3, pp 275-85.

Milligan, I. (2005) Mental health', in M. Smith (ed) *Secure in the knowledge: Perspectives on practice in secure accommodation*, Glasgow: Scottish Institute for Residential Child Care

Mitchell, R.C. (2005) 'Children's rights', in M. Smith (ed.) *Secure in the knowledge: Perspectives on practice in secure accommodation*, pp 246-51, Glasgow: Scottish Institute for Residential Child Care.

Moffitt, T.E., Caspi, A., Rutter, M., and Silva, P.A. (2001) *Sex differences in antisocial behaviour*, Cambridge: Cambridge University Press.

Moos, R.H. (1976) *The human context: Environmental determinants of behavior*, New York: John Wiley.

Morgan, R. (2006) 'Teachers "have lost courage to tackle bad behaviour"', *The Times*, 21 August.

Moss, P. and Petrie, P. (2002) *From children's services to children's spaces*, London: Routledge/Falmer.

Munro, E. (2011) *The Munro review of child protection: Final report: A child-centred system*, London: Department of Education.

Neill, A.S. (1966) *Summerhill*, Harmondsworth: Penguin.

Nettle, D. (2005. *Happiness: The science behind your smile*, Oxford: Oxford University Press.

NICE/SCIE (2010) 'Promoting the quality of life of looked after children and young people', http://publications.nice.org.uk/looked-after-children-and-young-people-ph28/foreword

Nicholson, D. and Artz, S. (2003) 'Preventing youthful offending: Where do we go from here?, *Relational Child and Youth Care Practice,* 16 (4): 32–46.

Niss, M. (1999) 'Achievement behaviour', *Readings in Child and Youth Care for South African Students: 2*, Cape Town: NACCW, pp 95–96, www.cyc-net.org/cyc-online.cycol-1105-niss.html

Noddings, N. (1984) *Caring: A feminine approach to ethics and moral education*, Berkeley, CA: University of California Press.

Noddings, N. (1992) The challenge to care in schools: an alternative approach to education, New York: Teachers College Press

Noddings, N. (2002a) *Starting at home: Caring and social policy*, Berkeley, CA: University of California Press.

Noddings, N. (2002b) *Educating moral people: A caring alternative to moral education*, New York: Teachers' College Press.

Noddings, N. (2003) *Happiness and education*, New York: Cambridge University Press.

Owen, C. (2003) 'Men in the nursery', in J. Brannen and P. Moss (eds) *Rethinking children's care*, Buckingham: Open University Press.

Palmer, P.J. (1998) *The courage to teach: Exploring the inner landscape of a teacher's life*, San Francisco: Jossey-Bass.

Parton, N. (1985) *The politics of child abuse*, Basingstoke: Macmillan

Payne, S. (1999) 'Poverty, social exclusion and mental health', working paper 15, *Poverty and Social Exclusion Survey of Britain*, Bristol: University of Bristol.

Perry, B and Szalavitz (2010) *Born for love: Why empathy is essential – and endangered*, New York: HarperCollins

Petrie, P. (2011) in Cameron, C. and Moss, P. (eds) (2011) *Social pedagogy and working with children and young people: Where care and education meet*, London: Jessica Kingsley Publishers.

Petrie, P. and Chambers, H. (2009) *Richer lives: Creative activities in the education and practice of Danish pedagogues. A preliminary study: Report to Arts Council England*, London: Thomas Coram Research Unit, Institute of Education, University of London.

Petrie, P., Boddy, J., Cameron, C., Wigfall, V. and Simon, A. (2006) *Working with children in care: European perspectives*, London: Open University Press.

Phelan, J. (1999) 'Experiments with experience', *Journal of Child and Youth Care Work*, vol 14, pp 25–8.

Phelan, J. (2001a) 'Another look at activities', *Journal of Child and Youth Care*, vol 14, no 2, pp 1–7, www.cyc-net.org/cyc-online/cycol-0107-phelan. html.

Phelan, J. (2001b) 'Experiential counselling and the CYC practitioner', *Journal of Child and Youth Care Work*, vols 15 and 16, special edition, pp 256–63.

Pinkney, S. (2011) 'Discourses of children's participation: professionals, policies and practices', *Social Policy and Society*, 10(03), pp 271–283.

Piper, H. and Stronach, I. (2008) *Don't touch! The educational story of a panic*, London: Routledge.

Pollitt, C. (1993) *Managerialism and the public services* (2nd edn), Oxford: Blackwell.

Powis, P., Allsopp, M. and Gannon, B. (1989) 'So the treatment plan', *The Child Care Worker*, vol 5, no 5, pp 3–4.

Punch, S., Dorrer, N., Emond, R. and McIntosh, I. (2009) *Food practices in residential children's homes: The views and experiences of staff and children*, Stirling: University of Stirling.

Putnam, R. (1995) 'Bowling alone: America's declining social capital'. *Journal of Democracy*, vol. 6 (1), 64-78.

Ramsden, I. (1997) 'Cultural safety: implementing the concept', in P. Te Whaiti, M. McCarthy and A. Durie (eds) *Mai i rangiatea: Maori wellbeing and development*, Auckland: Auckland University Press, pp 113–25.

Reclaiming Youth International (2012) www.reclaiming.com/content/about-circle-of-courage

Redl, F. (1966) *When we deal with children*, New York: The Free Press.

Redl, F. and Wineman, D. (1957) *The aggressive child*, New York: The Free Press.

Reeves, C. (ed) (2012) *Broken bounds: Contemporary reflections on the antisocial tendency*, London: Karnac.

Ricks, F. (1992) 'A feminist's view of caring', *Journal of Child and Youth Care,* vol 7, no 2, pp 49–57.

Ricks, F. and Bellefeuille, G. (2003) 'Knowing: the critical error of ethics in family work', in *A child and youth care approach to working with families*, ed. T. Garfat, Haworth: New York, pp 117-130.

Roosevelt, E. (1958) Presentation to the United Nations Commission on Human Rights, United Nations, New York, www.udhr.org/history/Biographies/bioer.htm

Rose, J. (2010) *How nurture protects children*, London: Responsive Solutions.

Rowe, J. and Lambert, L. (1973) *Children who wait: A study of children needing substitute families*, London: British Association for Adoption and Fostering.

Ruch G., Turney D. and Ward, A. (eds) (2010) *Relationship based social work: Getting to the heart of practice,* London: Jessica Kingsley Publishers.

Scottish Executive (2005) 'Getting it right for every child – proposals for action', Edinburgh: Scottish Executive

Scottish Executive (2006) *Changing lives: Report of the 21st Century Social Work Review,* Edinburgh: Scottish Executive.

Scottish Government (2007) *Looked after children and young people: We can and must do better,* www.scotland.gov.uk/Publications/2007/01/15084446/0

Scottish Government (2008) *These are our bairns: A guide for community planning partnerships on being a good corporate parent,* www.scotland.gov.uk/Publications/2008/08/29115839/0

SCRA (Scottish Children's Reporter Administration) (2004) *Social backgrounds of children referred to the reporter: A pilot study,* Stirling: SCRA.

Seligman, M.E.P. (1992) *Helplessness: On depression, development, and death,* New York: Freeman.

Seligman, M.E.P. (2002) *Authentic happiness: Using the new positive psychology to realize your potential for lasting fulfillment,* New York: Free Press.

Sen, R., Kendrick, A., Milligan, I. and Hawthorn, M. (2008) 'Lessons learnt? Abuse in residential child care in Scotland', *Child and Family Social Work,* vol 13, no 4, pp 411–22.

Sevenhuijsen, S. (1998) *Citizenship and the ethics of care: Feminist considerations on justice, morality, and politics,* London: Routledge.

Sharpe, C. (2006) 'Residential child care and the psychodynamic approach: is it time to try again?', *Scottish Journal of Residential Child Care,* vol 5, no 1, pp 46–56.

Sikes, P. and Piper, H. (2010) *Researching sex and lies in the classroom: Allegations of sexual misconduct in schools,* London: Routledge.

Simon, J. and Smith, L.T. (2001) *A civilising mission? Perceptions and representations of the New Zealand native schools system,* Auckland: Auckland University Press.

Smart, M. (2010) Generosity, learning and residential child care, Goodenoughcaring.com/Journal/Article139.htm

Smith, D. J. and McAra, L. (2004) 'Gender and youth offending', *Edinburgh study of youth transitions and crime research,* digest no 2.

Smith, H. and Smith, M.K. (2008) *The art of helping others: Being around, being there, being wise,* London: Jessica Kingsley Publishers.

Smith, M. (2008) 'The other side of the story', *CYC-Online,* issue 114, www.cyc-net.org/cyc-online/cyconline-aug2008-smith.html

Smith, M. (2009) *Re-thinking residential child care: Positive perspectives,* Bristol: The Policy Press.

Smith, M. (2010a) 'Victim narratives of historical abuse in residential child care: do we really know what we think we know?', *Qualitative Social Work,* vol 9, no 3, pp 303–20.

Smith, M. (2010b) 'Gender in residential child care', in B. Featherstone, C.-A. Hooper, J. Scourfield and J. Taylor (eds) *Gender and child welfare in society*, Oxford: Wiley-Blackwell.

Smith, M. (2011a) 'Love and the child and youth care relationship', *Relational Child and Youth Care Practice*, vol 24, no 1/2, pp 189–93.

Smith, M. (2011b) 'Reading Bauman for social work', *Ethics and Social Welfare*, vol 5, no 1, pp 2–17.

Smith, M. (2012) 'Theory in residential child care work', in M. Davies (ed) *Social work with children and families*, Basingstoke: Palgrave Macmillan.

Smith, M., Cree, V. and Clapton, G. (2012) 'Time to be heard: interrogating the Scottish Government's response to historical child abuse', *Scottish Affairs*, Winter 2012.

Smith, M., McKay, E. and Chakrabarti, M. (2004) 'What works for us – boys' views of their experiences in a former list D school', *British Journal of Special Education*, vol 31, no 2, pp 89–94.

Steckley, L. (2005) 'Just a game? The therapeutic potential of football', in D. Crimmens and I. Milligan, *Facing the future: Residential child care in the 21st century*, Lyme Regis: Russell House Publishing.

Steckley, L. (2009) 'Don't touch', *CYC-Online*, issue 130, www.cyc-net.org/cyc-online/cyconline-dec2009-steckley.html

Steckley, L. (2010) 'Containment and holding environments: understanding and reducing physical restraint in residential child care', *Children and Youth Services Review*, vol 32, no 1, pp 120–8.

Steckley, L. (2012) 'Touch, physical restraint and therapeutic containment in residential child care', *British Journal of Social Work,* advance online access published July 7, 2011.

Steckley, L. and Kendrick, A. (2005) 'Physical restraint in residential child care: the experiences of young people and residential workers', *Children and Youth in Emerging and Transforming Societies International Conference*, Oslo, 29 June–3 July.

Steckley, L. and Smith, M. (2011) 'Care ethics in residential child care: a different voice' *Ethics and Social Welfare*, vol 5, no 2, pp 181–95.

Stevens, I. Kirkpatrick, R. and McNicol, C. (2008) 'Improving literacy though storytelling in residential care', *Scottish Journal of Residential Child Care,* special edition: education, vol 7, no 2, pp 28–40.

Stewart, T. (1997) 'Historical interfaces between Maori and psychology', in P. Te Whaiti, M. McCarthy and A. Durie (eds) *Mai i rangiatea: Maori wellbeing and development,* Auckland: Auckland University Press, pp 75–95.

Stremmel, A. J. (1993) 'Introduction: implications of Vygotsky's sociocultural theory for child and youth care practice', *Child and Youth Care Forum*, vol 22, no 5, pp 333–5.

Sutton Trust (2010) *Education mobility in England: The link between the education levels of parents and the educational outcomes of teenagers,* www.suttontrust.com/research/education-mobility-in-england/

Swinton, J. (2005) *Why psychiatry needs spirituality,* www.rcpsych.ac.uk/pdf/ATT89153.ATT.pdf

Tavecchio, L. (2003) Presentation at the 'Men in Childcare' conference, Belfry, Ghent, November

Taylor, C. (2006) *Young people in care and criminal behaviour,* London: Jessica Kingsley Publishers.

Te Whaiti, P., McCarthy, M. and Durie A. (eds) *Mai i rangiatea: Maori wellbeing and development,* Auckland: Auckland University Press.

Thin, N. (2009) *Schoolchildren's wellbeing and life prospects: Justifying the universal tax on childhood (WeD Working Paper 09/46),* Bath: University of Bath.

Trieschman, A. (1982) 'The anger within' [videotape interview], Washington, DC: NAK Productions.

Trieschman, A., Whittaker, J.K. and Brendtro, L.K. (1969) *The other 23 hours: Child-care work with emotionally disturbed children in a therapeutic milieu,* New York: Aldine De Gruiter.

Tritter, J.Q. and McCallum, A. (2006) 'The snakes and ladders of user involvement: moving beyond Arnstein', *Health Policy,* vol 76, pp 156–168.

Tronto, J. (1994) *Moral boundaries: A political argument for an ethic of care,* London: Routledge.

Tutu, D (n/d) 'Ubuntu', www.catholicsocialteaching.org.uk/themes/human-dignity/

Trotter, C. (1999) *Working with involuntary clients: A guide to practice,* London: Sage Publications.

UNICEF (2007) *An overview of child well-being in rich countries,* Florence: UNICEF

VanderVen, K. (1999) 'You are what you do and become what you've done: the role of activity in development of self', *Journal of Child and Youth Care,* vol 13 no 2, pp 133–47.

VanderVen, K. (2003) 'Bedtime story, a wake up call – and serve it with a cup of cocoa', *International Child and Youth Care Network,* no 51, www.cyc-net.org/cyc-online/cycol-0403-karen.html

VanderVen, K. (2005) 'Transforming the milieu and lives through the power of activity: theory and practice', *Cyc-online,* no 82, www.cyc-net.org/cyc-online/cycol-1105-vanderven.html

Vanier, J. (2001) *Made for happiness: Discovering the meaning of life with Aristotle,* London: Dartman, Longman, Todd.

Ward, A. (1993) *Working in group care,* Birmingham: Venture Press.

Ward, A. (1995) 'The impact of parental suicide on children and staff in residential care: a case study in the function of containment', *Journal of Social Work Practice,* vol 9, no 1, pp 23–32.

Waterhouse, R. (2000) *Lost in care,* London: The Stationery Office.

Webb, D. (2010) 'A certain moment: some personal reflections on aspects of residential childcare in the 1950s', *British Journal of Social Work,* vol 40, no 5, pp 1387–401.

Webb, S. (2006) *Social work in a risk society: Social and political perspectives,* Basingstoke: Palgrave.

Webster, R. (2005) *The secret of Bryn Estyn: The making of a modern witch hunt,* Oxford: The Orwell Press.

Whan, M. (1986) 'On the nature of practice', *British Journal of Social Work,* vol 16, no 2, pp 243–50.

White, K. J. (2008) *The growth of love: Understanding the five essential elements of child development,* Abingdon: The Bible Reading Fellowship.

Whittaker, J.K. (1979) *Caring for troubled children,* San Francisco: Jossey-Bass

Whyte, B. (2009) *Youth justice in practice: Making a difference,* Bristol: The Policy Press.

Wilkinson, R. and Pickett, K. (2009) *The spirit level: Why more equal societies almost always do better,* London: Allen Lane.

Winnicott, D.W. (1965) *Maturational processes and the facilitating environment,* London: Hogarth Press

Wolfensberger, W. (1980) The definition of normalisation: update, problems, disagreements and misunderstandings. In R.J. Flynn and K.E. Nitsch (eds) *Normalization, social integration and human services,* Baltimore: University Park Press

Wright, P., Turner, C., Clay, D. and Mills, H. (2006) *The participation of children and young people in developing social care,* London: Social Care Institute for Excellence.

Index